Inspire, Empower, Connect

Inspire, Empower, Connect

Reaching across Cultural Differences to Make a Real Difference

Anne Chan

ROWMAN & LITTLEFIELD EDUCATION

A division of

ROWMAN & LITTLEFIELD PUBLISHERS, INC.
Lanham • New York • Toronto • Plymouth, UK

Published by Rowman & Littlefield Education
A division of Rowman & Littlefield Publishers, Inc.
A wholly owned subsidary of The Rowman & Littlefield Publishing Group, Inc.
4501 Forbes Boulevard, Suite 200, Lanham, Maryland 20706
http://www.rowmaneducation.com

Estover Road
Plymouth PL6 7PY
United Kingdom

British Library Cataloguing in Publication Information Available

Library of Congress Cataloging-in-Publication Data

Chan, Anne, 1968-
  Inspire, empower, connect : reaching across cultural differences to make a real
difference / by Anne Chan.
    p. cm.
  Includes bibliographical references.
  ISBN 978-1-60709-603-0 (cloth : alk. paper) — ISBN 978-1-60709-604-7 (pbk. : alk.
paper) — ISBN 978-1-60709-605-4 (electronic)
  1. Mentoring.   2. Multiculturalism.   I. Title.
  BF637.M45C43 2010
  158'.3—dc22   2009033088

Printed in the United States of America

∞™ The paper used in this publication meets the minimum requirements of American
National Standard for Information Sciences—Permanence of Paper for Printed Library
Materials, ANSI/NISO Z39.48-1992.

Contents

Contents

Acknowledgments

It took the support of a village and many mentors to help me write and finish this book. I am deeply grateful, honored, and appreciative of every one who believed in me and encouraged me through the process.

To my husband, Andrew, who unwaveringly cheered me on, gave me all the emotional and technical support I needed, was the unending source of love, support, encouragement, and acceptance, and who cheerfully took turns to take care of our little one—I can always lean on you, even when your leg was broken. I am deeply appreciative of your presence in my life.

To Joe White, mentor of mentors. I will always be humbled, grateful, and appreciative that you took me under your wing and consistently showed caring, kindness, and concern. Without you, I would not even have known about mentoring and would not have dreamed I could write a book about mentoring. You inspired this book . . . you always inspire me to be a better person and humanitarian.

My deepest thanks to my research participants who so generously shared with me their thoughts, ideas, and experiences of mentoring. This book would not exist without you. Thank you for teaching, enlightening, and inspiring me.

To Carl and Linda, my in-laws from heaven—you have been steadfastly by my side from the very beginning. Your love and support mean more to me than you could ever know.

To Peg Boyle Single—your friendship and mentoring were essential in helping me birth this baby! Thank you for believing in me and in my work, and in providing guidance, friendship, feedback, and support whenever I needed it.

To Pam—friend, soul sister, kindred spirit—our e-friendship has meant the world to me.

To Frankie—it was an honor for me to have you proof-read this book. Thank you for your eagle eyes and unconditional support.

To Sherry—thank you for answering my thousand and one questions about graphic design!

Last but not least, to Aren. Thank you for putting up with a Mom whose attention was sometimes diverted by this other bookish sibling. You are always in my heart. Just know that I wrote this book from the deepest heart-felt conviction that love supports, nurtures, and lasts forever.

Foreword

I started mentoring since I was a child, but I didn't call it "mentoring" back then. When I started preschool, my mother called me the Pied Piper because there were always kids following me and I was showing them how to do Math, spelling, and writing. I lived in a very poor neighborhood and there were children who didn't have money for lunch, so I would give them my lunch money. In turn, the other children in the class saw me giving my lunch money away and they gave me their extra money or food. It didn't cost me anything extra to give of myself. I always got my lunch and everybody got fed.

When I was fourteen, I learned a lesson about mentoring that has stayed with me ever since. That year, I was all set to win THE prize as the best camper at senior camp. It was my goal and I believed I earned it since I was captain of the basketball and track team, president of the camp council and editor of the newspaper. I was Mr. Everybody at the camp and thought the prize was a slam-dunk.

My mother warned me not to count my chickens before they hatched. She was right – they awarded the prize to another boy. I was so heart broken and mad I got up in the middle of the night and went out in the woods and cried and cussed. One evening, the camp director sat me down and looked me straight in the eye and said, "You won the prize, Joe, but the other boy deserved it." He explained that the other boy's mom had died, his dad was drinking a lot and he was trying to take care of his younger brothers and sisters. He said this other boy needed the affirmation and the prize.

The director then said something to me that I initially struggled with, but have subsequently lived by for the rest of my life. He said, "Joe, you've been blessed with everything. You've got a mother who loves you. You're good looking. You're the most popular kid around here. You're smart. You've got everything going for you and you weren't given all of this just for yourself. You were given this so you could go out in the world and help other people. If you help them, you'll get your share. You don't need to be worrying about that. You will get your share!"

He was basically trying to tell me that if I gave, I would receive. But his message confused me because I'd always been taught to compete to be Number One and not worry about anybody else other than myself. Yet, this camp director was saying the exact opposite—he was trying to tell me that when I made others Number One, then I'd be fine.

It's been many years since my camp director said those words to me. I am now in my seventh decade of life and it turns out the camp director was right. Whenever I mentored and facilitated others, my career expanded and everything worked fine in my life. Whenever I turned my back on others and got tired of helping people, my life went off track.

I am enriched by the very fact of giving and I have grown immeasurably through the process of mentoring others. With every successful relationship I enter with other human beings, their richness eventually flows into me just as mine flows into them. The other benefit I get is to watch the growth process and know I had some part in the success of others. Like a farmer, I plant a seed in the ground and water it and hope the sun shines. I do whatever I think will help it grow, and then I step back and watch it begin to grow. It's a fascinating process and I'm in the flow of knowledge building, creating, being part of what is unfolding, and of having first witnessed it in its embryonic form.

When I started out in my career, I and other Black psychologists wanted to change the field of psychology. We initially tried to change psychology by confrontation. Then it dawned on me that one of the ways to change psychology was to get more talented people into it so that each of them would do a little something to create change. Our individual and collective efforts to mentor the best and brightest into psychology has resulted in resoundingly positive outcomes for ethnic minority psychology. Ethnic minorities in psychology have made strides far beyond what I could have imagined or hoped for when I began my career.

Now when I attend conferences and see scholars and students advancing the boundaries of multicultural psychology, I feel satisfaction knowing that I was a part of many of these people at one stage or another of their lives. They're creating monumental political and organizational change. This profound change in the epistemology of knowledge and of psychology began when we all worked together and connected with each other rather than competing against each other.

Lots of people talk about mentoring and want to mentor. Just as many people talk about multiculturalism and increasing diversity. Unfortunately, although these buzzwords are used all the time, most people do not know what they mean in terms of actual practice and action. Dr. Chan's book, *Inspire, Connect, Empower,* fills the gap by showing what goes on in a mentoring relationship and what mentors actually do with their protégés. Dr. Chan takes mentors by the hand through all the basics of mentoring and through the thorny issues of cross-racial and cross-cultural differences in mentoring relationships. Her gentle guidance shows us how such differences can be handled successfully.

Dr. Chan explains how we can reach across cultural differences and have satisfying and productive relationships with people very different from us. I wholeheartedly agree with her on the need for people to learn how to connect and build trust. My definition of mentoring starts with the connectedness between two human beings. When connectedness is established, the mentor and protégé can then begin to build a relationship. It is critical and essential to set the foundations for a mentoring relationship where protégés feel secure and confident so they can open up. Trust is developed slowly by accomplishing little steps in the relationship. Mentors have to know that trust develop through spending time together and telling stories. You simply cannot sit down with a brand new protégé and expect automatic trust by saying, "Trust me."

This book is an important resource book for anyone who wants to work effectively and successfully with people they encounter at their workplaces, community organizations, schools, colleges, churches, mosques, temples, and volunteer settings. You *can* make a real difference whether you are a higher education faculty, advisor, teacher, guidance counselor, student services personnel, school administrator, professional, church-goer, supervisor, boss, or project manager. You *can* make a significant impact on anyone you meet, whether they are school kids, college students, graduate students, employees, volunteers, colleagues or peers.

If you are the head of a department or president of an organization, read this book and give copies to your teachers, staff, and employees so they can learn to mentor each other and transform the school or work environment in the process. We often talk about lofty goals like raising achievement scores, increasing minority recruitment and workplace productivity—Dr. Chan provides the method and the practical strategies for achieving these positive outcomes through mentoring.

Just as I worked to transform the field of psychology, so can you change the world around you, one person at a time. Anyone can mentor if they have the desire and the skills to help others. With this book as your guide, you will learn and understand the skills required of successful mentors. I've always told Dr. Chan to pass it on, and she has done so through her research and publication of this book on mentoring. Now the baton is in your hands—start mentoring and make a real difference in people's lives!

Joseph L. White, PhD
Professor Emeritus of Psychology and Psychiatry,
University of California, Irvine
Coauthor of *Black Man Emerging* and
Building Multicultural Competency

Introduction

We make an odd looking pair, my mentor and I, when we are together at conferences. Joe is an African American elder with grizzled salt and pepper hair and a powerful stride, whereas I'm a short, middle-aged Chinese woman who prefers to blend into the background. Joe exudes a gregarious warmth when he enters a room and hails a hearty greeting to everyone, "How ya'll doing?" The energy in the room immediately revs up several notches. He is a human magnet, literally drawing people in with the irresistible force of his personality and charm. In sharp contrast, I'm shy, reserved, much more guarded, and easily intimidated. I abhor the limelight and actually *like* watching from the sidelines. I would never dream of calling out to a crowd of strangers and would rather walk barefoot on cut glass than go networking.

With all these differences between us, it is unbelievable that we have anything to say to each other, let alone enjoy a close relationship. We diverge in a multitude of areas, including:

- gender—he's male, I'm female
- race—he's African American, I'm Asian American
- country of origin—he's American, I was born in Singapore
- immigration history—I'm a recent immigrant to America, he's not
- family background—he was from a single-parent household; I grew up in a two-parent household
- personal history and experiences—he was actively involved in the Civil Rights movement whereas I was born at the height of the movement
- age—he is almost twice my age

Despite these many differences, our relationship is one of genuine caring, support, respect, understanding, authenticity, and connectedness. I credit much of the success of our relationship to Joe's finesse in mentoring.

The fact that I became his protégé speaks to his tremendous abilities in reaching out and creating mentoring relationships with diverse people.

Back in 2000, my advisor casually recommended I attend a national multicultural conference. All I remember him saying was, "Go to the conference and say 'Hi' to Joe." I had no idea who this "Joe" was. I arrived at the conference and discovered, to my shock, that "Joe" was by no means an average Joe. On the contrary, he was to be honored at this conference for his lifetime contributions to psychology. Not only had he trained thousands of psychologists as a professor at the University of California, Irvine, he had also single-handedly transformed the field of psychology with his work on Black psychology.

My fear of meeting him tripled—I figured someone of his stature wouldn't have the time of day for me. Magnifying my fear was my feeling completely out of place at this conference. I did not know anyone and was not affiliated with an academic institution. I tried to introduce myself to people, but their lack of interest was painfully evident by the way they scanned the room for someone else to talk to. I was not enjoying the conference, and the thought of meeting Joe intensified my dread.

I consoled myself with the thought that I would greet him as quickly as I could, bail the conference, then reward myself with an ice-cream sundae. My escape plan was thwarted when Joe gave such an electrifying speech that he received a standing ovation and was mobbed by an adoring crowd. I inched my 5'3" frame past the mob of people just to get close to him. I had no idea what to say. I timidly stammered out my name and told him who had sent me, fully expecting him to give me a perfunctory nod and turn to the next person. To my amazement, Joe did not conveniently brush me aside. Instead, he gave me a big smile, greeted me warmly, took me by the arm, and invited me to join him at his lunch table. I was flabbergasted by his unexpected kindness.

Prior to meeting him, I felt like a nobody at that conference, but Joe treated me like I was a Somebody. He took me under his wing, then sat with me and talked to me about my goals and dreams. I remember telling him I was applying to different doctoral programs across the country, but was nervous about leaving California because of my husband's desire to stay in the Golden State. He listened carefully, with genuine interest. My plans, worries, and insecurities mattered to him. After our time together, he took my information and said he'd be in touch.

My prior experience with other people made me distrust his word. I thought that our meeting was amazing, but assumed he would forget me, go on with his life and more important lifework, and that would be that. Little did I know that this encounter would forever change the direction as well as the quality of my professional and personal life.

A few weeks later, I received a handwritten letter in Joe's confident scrawl:

> Dear Anne,
> Enjoyed the opportunity to chat with you in California. Keep me updated on your decision making as the opportunities unfold. Dropped note to R. in the Psychology Dept. Be sure to tell him you know me. He can tell you all about New York. My daughter Lois sends regards.
> Keep the faith.
> Joe White
> P.S. I think you have a bright future ahead.

I was stunned when I received his note—Joe's word was good when he said he would keep in touch. I began to believe that he really meant it when he said he wanted to mentor me.

From that meeting on, he checked with me once a week on Sunday evenings. My Sundays with Joe were, I daresay, as good as Tuesdays with Morrie. By initiating these phone calls, he made contact possible. He knew I would never have had the nerve to call him, so he proactively called me instead. His calls proved to me that he really cared, and as we got to know each other, our conversations supported the growth of our relationship.

I was both struck and gratified that he was open about himself, both personally and professionally. He always said just the right amount so I would know enough about him, but not so much that he was foisting his concerns onto me.

I am admittedly not a trusting person. I warm up to people just about as speedily as a snail finishes a marathon. However, I quickly grew to trust Joe because he explicitly demonstrated his caring, he was proactive about initiating and maintaining contact, his word was always good, and he showed interest in and caring for me. I did not see much of him during my entire doctoral program since we live far apart. However, distance did not matter in our relationship because his gestures maintained my trust.

There are some things that Joe gives me that no one else in my life can provide, no matter how loving, caring, and supportive they are. One special and unique aspect about our relationship is that I think of him very specifically as my mentor. Although I certainly feel friendship, caring, and support from him, I do not perceive him as a friend or a family member. Rather, I identify him as an elder in the profession who is my guide and champion. The word "mentor" best captures the essence of my relationship with him. Joe freely provides mentoring in these important areas:

Professional and Career Development

- gives advice and input into my career direction
- gives me opportunities to develop my career
- introduces me to a professional community and strengthens my professional alliances
- gives me insight into his personal and professional experiences as an African American psychologist and academic
- gives me the inside scoop on how the profession works
- teaches me the tricks of the trade
- provides answers to my questions regarding the profession
- provides practical help and resources to enhance my career

Personal Development

- inspires me
- acts as a role model
- is a trusted person I can turn to for support, help, and guidance
- protects me
- serves as a sounding board

Integration of Personal and Career Development

- understands my multiple roles and identities and helps me integrate key aspects of my life and career
- supports my development and growth as a woman, a person of color, a mother, a writer, a researcher, a teacher, a psychotherapist, a consultant, and a professional

Good mentors strive to fulfill many of the roles listed above. However, Joe is exceptional for his holistic approach to mentoring. In our conversations he synergistically blends the personal and professional, attending to my multiple, sometimes competing professional and personal identities. And always, always, always, he is sensitive to the fact and the implications of what it means to be a person of color in a profession that is largely Euro-American.

My relationship with Joe is a nexus of cross-cultural differences. However, it would not be accurate to say that our relationship transcends differences. Rather, there is a welcoming and embracing of our differences so that they are openly and seamlessly interwoven into our relationship. Each of us recognizes and appreciates the differences that could potentially divide us. Our relationship is richer, more interesting, and infinitely more satisfying to me because we have connected through our differences.

I know that Joe recognizes the multiple intricacies of my life and my history. I appreciate that he does not see me as a one-dimensional being, but rather understands the complexity of the various parts that create the whole that is me. In turn, I appreciate and respect his lifetime of challenges living as a Black man in America and working as a minority pioneer in the field of psychology.

When I think of the cross-cultural relationship I have with Joe, I feel hope for the future, for people successfully bridging differences that typically divide. If Joe and I can have a mutually enriching, satisfying, and supportive relationship that is inclusive of each other's background, then so can others.

As the lucky recipient of Joe's mentoring, I can attest to the power of mentoring. I may well have dropped out of my doctoral program without Joe's consistent support and guidance. I have become empowered, strengthened, and enriched in a myriad of ways beyond my ability to count. I would not have written this book if not for Joe's encouragement, help, and support. I would not even have *known* about mentoring if not for Joe.

If you are still wondering why you should bother to mentor, read on. Many research studies have shown that mentoring is associated with numerous benefits, including greater career satisfaction, more promotions, higher salaries, less isolation, stronger self-efficacy, easier socialization, greater productivity, and increased commitment to a profession and organization. Boyle and Boice (1998) write: "Mentorship may be the most important variable related to academic and career success for graduate students" (p. 90). Other scholars have underscored the critical importance of mentoring for success in business, medicine, education, psychology, and other fields.

Joe's inspirational mentoring of me and many others has compelled me to write this book. Joe's legacy of mentoring is formidable—he has personally mentored over 100 PhDs. Yet, Joe is just one person. More people need to step up so that everyone who needs a mentor can benefit from exemplary mentoring.

Joe never asked for anything in return; instead he asked me to pass it on. This book is my attempt to pass it on. I have done my best to distill Joe's mentoring magic and share it with everyone else.

The strategies in this book are based primarily on my pilot and dissertation research studies of outstanding mentors and their protégés, as well as on current research on mentoring. My research focused on in-depth studies of exemplary, cross-cultural relationships, involving interviews with mentors and their protégés, analysis of actual mentoring sessions, as well as an examination of their e-mail exchanges. I devoted over three years of my life to this research in order to understand what these mentors did to create and sustain such mutually satisfying and productive relationships, even in the midst of stark differences. The case examples given in this book are loosely based on participants in my research studies—I have altered identifying details so as to protect their privacy. However, I have used the actual words and e-mails of the mentors and protégés I interviewed to give you real-life reports of different mentoring experiences.

I felt honored to interview these outstanding mentors and their protégés. In a troubling world where conflict, hatred, and violence pervade the news, it was simultaneously encouraging, inspiring, and comforting to witness relationships where mutual support and deep caring were the recurring themes.

I believe that many people earnestly want to mentor and make a difference in other people's lives, but they often do not know how. They rightly get concerned about how to connect with someone who is from a different background. They might ask, "What do I have in common with someone who comes from a different culture or a different country?" Or, "I grew up in the suburbs—how do I mentor someone who grew up in the hood?"

This book will give you the answers to these questions by illustrating and explaining the components of exemplary mentoring. It will teach you how to be an outstanding mentor and how to make a difference in other people's lives, while at the same time helping them feel completely accepted and validated for who they are. You will learn how to identify, talk about, and even embrace differences so that you can become a standout mentor.

You can use these mentoring techniques in a variety of ways. Some of you might be inspired to start an intensive one-on-one relationship, like Joe did with me. Others might sign up for a Big Brothers or Big Sisters program. If this is too daunting, you can be an e-mentor.

Or you could incorporate some of the techniques described in this book in your daily interactions with others. Even adopting one or two of these strategies will help you reach across racial, cultural, and other divides and make a difference in someone else's life. If you're an advisor or a counselor, you can enhance your encounters with your advisees by using a few of the tools described here. If you're a classroom teacher, you can experiment with the techniques in a group setting. If you're a supervisor, try integrating some of the techniques in your management style. These techniques will take your advising, counseling, and managing competences to an exemplary level.

I write this book with the hope that you will be inspired to mentor. My wish is that this book will encourage, empower, and equip you with the knowledge, awareness, and confidence to reach out to others who look, act, believe, or talk differently.

You *can* make a difference, even in the midst of real differences.

FOCUS OF THIS BOOK

This book outlines what mentors can do to foster a successful relationship. Note that the emphasis in this book is on *doing* rather than on being. I will illustrate and explain the strategies a mentor can take, rather than describe the qualities needed in a mentor.

Of course, mentors generally share personal qualities such as being caring, compassionate, and sensitive. However, the focus of this book is the "how to" of mentoring—how to demonstrate your caring, compassion, sensitivity, and how to translate these qualities into action, particularly in cross-race and cross-cultural relationships. The reason for this particular focus is to give you clear, achievable steps you can take when you mentor. This is a deliberately practical approach that will give you concrete tools and ideas for mentoring. I guarantee that using these tools with your protégé will deepen and enrich your mentoring relationship.

The focus on mentor practices does not mean that protégés need not contribute anything to the relationship. Quite the contrary—a whole other book could be written on what protégés need to do to maintain a successful mentoring relationship. Protégés, too, need to step up to the plate, do their part, and contribute to the success of the relationship. Here's a short list of the key qualities protégés need in order to have a successful mentoring relationship:

- be responsive
- have good follow-through
- be open to feedback
- be willing to be guided and mentored
- be open about self, including personal strengths and weaknesses

A WORD ON RACE AND CULTURE

There are no universally accepted definitions for the words *race, culture,* and *ethnicity*. Although these are not scientific constructs, I use them because they are meaningful to those who either self-identify or are categorized along these lines. I encourage you to ask your protégés what these concepts mean to them and how they affect their lives. Here is a quick guide to the terminology used in this book but bear in mind that these terms hold different meanings for different people:

Race refers to the broad racial categories often used in a census form, for example, Asian American, Native American, African American, or European American. Race is usually based on physical characteristics.

Ethnicity refers to a shared heritage that is based on various factors, such as religion, national or geographical origin.

Culture/Cultural are broad terms that refer to a group sharing values, beliefs, practices, and ideas.

The majority of mentoring relationships, even ones where mentor and protégé appear similar on the surface, contain differences that can potentially hinder understanding. For example, two European American women from the same city and going to the same college might differ sharply in their socioeconomic status, generation, and religious beliefs.

In getting to know your protégé, take a good look at the racial/ethnic/cultural ways where you differ and where you are alike (see Checklist, Table 6.1, pg. 29)

HOW TO USE THIS BOOK

This book is organized around the three main areas that constitute outstanding mentoring: (1) building trust, (2) developing the protégé's skills, knowledge, and competencies, and (3) facilitating the socialization of the protégé. Each of the chapters that follows highlights an essential mentor practice within each of these three areas. I give a case example of each practice, an explanation of why the practice matters, and practical strategies for implementing the practice in your mentoring relationship. When appropriate, I have provided practical strategies targeted for specific groups, such as school-aged children, teachers in training, and workforce protégés.

If you are in a hurry or simply want to focus on the "how-to" of mentoring, review the next chapter, *The Big Picture,* then turn to the last section of each chapter to get concrete ideas for different ways you can put each mentor practice into action.

Doing any *one* of these practices can make a difference in a person's life. I encourage you to choose one or more of the practices outlined in this book and try them out on a colleague, supervisee, friend, child, or even a stranger. You'll see how much positive change you can enact in a person's life simply by doing even *one* of these mentoring practices.

Doing several or even all of these practices will make a profound impact in your protégé's life and will create a mentoring relationship that is deeply meaningful, satisfying, and productive for both of you.

The outstanding mentors in my research studies made a tremendous impact in their protégés' personal and professional lives by doing these simple, yet effective practices.

So can you.

Chapter 1

The Big Picture

What Effective Mentoring Looks Like

There are as many definitions of mentoring as there are ways to mentor—you can mentor a group, a child, adult, student, or supervisee. You can be a peer mentor or even an e-mentor to someone you have never set eyes on.

Although mentoring contains the same elements of friendship, supervision, and support common in many types of relationships, it is qualitatively different from being someone's friend, lover, boss, spouse, therapist, significant other, teacher, or parent.

What sets a mentoring relationship apart are the following distinctive qualities and features:

- The basis and purpose of the relationship is the guiding, advising, and supporting of the protégé's growth.
- There is caring, mutual respect, trust, and regard in both parties.
- There is transfer and sharing of information, tips, and expertise in the process of mentoring.
- The mentor helps the protégé learn and integrate into a new role or stage of personal, academic, or professional development.

"GOOD" VS. "BAD" MENTORING

Even though mentoring is based on the premise of supporting and helping the protégé, mentoring relationships can vary greatly in quality. As a mentor, you can be deeply caring or indifferent. You can mentor for a quick moment in time or sustain a mentoring relationship through an entire lifespan. Some mentors, unfortunately, believe they are operating with the best of intentions, but may be abusive in their actions.

The focus of this book is on the very best of mentoring. I'm not interested in describing how to be an average or passable mentor. I want to give you the tools to be an outstanding mentor, and to learn how to make a meaningful and successful connection with another person, even when differences divide.

In order to be an outstanding mentor, you need to understand three things about mentoring across cultural differences:

#1 Key Point: The Relationship Matters

There is special significance in my use of the word "relationship" to describe what happens between mentor and protégé.

I intentionally use the word *relationship* because my research showed clearly that the most mutually meaningful, satisfying, and productive mentoring experiences were ones where both mentors and protégés acknowledged that they had a true relationship.

These clearly weren't standard workplace acquaintanceships or casual encounters. Instead, these were relationships that were real, meaningful, and significant to both mentors and protégés. Both sides had a deep commitment to the relationship. Both enjoyed a definite bond of caring, trust, respect, and regard. The majority of the protégés saw their mentoring relationships as life-long. One of the mentoring pairs I interviewed had known each other for over eleven years, and they continue to talk on the phone and e-mail each other at least three times a week to this day.

Granted, you can have a mentoring moment—a quick snapshot in time where you help someone out, listen, give advice, and inspire. You give them what they need in that precious moment, then both of you move on and a true relationship does not develop.

These mentoring moments can be meaningful and memorable, but they do not constitute a real relationship.

In contrast, a mentoring relationship is a personal relationship where there's genuine caring, sharing, participation, and commitment.

So when you think about mentoring, reflect on the importance of creating a relationship that is real and that matters.

#2 Key Point: Three Areas of Mentoring and the Importance of Trust

To have a truly outstanding mentoring relationship, there are three main areas that the mentor has to attend to:

1. Establish trust and build a genuine relationship with the protégé.
2. Develop the protégé's personal and professional/academic skills.

3. Facilitate the protégé's socialization and integration into communities that matter to the protégé, whether it's the school, college, or workplace.

These three areas of mentor practices often occur simultaneously, one blending into another. A single mentoring session is likely to touch on two or even all three areas at the same time. For instance, discussing how to make a speech can also help socialize the protégé into school or work.

The mentor practices in this book are organized around these three areas. Although each of the three areas is vital for a fully successful, satisfying, and productive mentoring relationship, the importance of building trust between you and your protégé cannot be overemphasized, particularly when cross-cultural differences are involved.

Trust is a vital component in the development and maintenance of a true mentoring relationship. It is simply not enough to have a desire to help. Trust has to be established before your protégés will let you into their lives and accept your help.

The following section lays out the fundamentals of how to earn your protégé's trust. These practices are especially critical if you want to create a healthy, helping relationship with someone culturally different from yourself.

If you have earned your protégés' trust and have successfully conveyed that you understand, support, and care about them, then they are more likely to:

- divulge their vulnerabilities, challenges, and setbacks
- turn to you when they need support or advice
- entrust you with their lives, dreams, and hopes
- be open about themselves
- feel supported and cared for
- welcome you into their lives
- ask you for help
- accept your support and help

In cross-cultural and cross-racial relationships, trust is likely to develop more slowly because of historic tensions or suspicions. Johnson-Bailey and Cervero (2002) eloquently state this problem:

On the surface, the concept of trust as it applies to mentoring appears simplistic: it needs to be reciprocal in nature and it's a matter between the mentor and protégé. However, in cross-cultural mentoring what should be a simple matter of negotiation between two persons becomes an arbitration between historical legacies, contemporary racial tensions, and societal protocols. A cross-cultural mentoring relationship is an affiliation between unequals who are conducting their relationship on a hostile American stage, with a societal script contrived to undermine the success of the partnership (p. 18).

In cross-race and cross-cultural relationships, the development of trust and the solidifying of the relationship become not only necessary, but critical for mentoring success. This is why the area of relationship- and trust-building is highlighted first in this book. Mentors paired with protégés different from themselves must be knowledgeable about the impediments to building trust. They must be comfortable as well as patient in working towards earning the trust of their protégés.

#3 Key Point: Understand the Complexity of Your Protégé's World

There should be a warning sign that comes to any individual, group, organization, or nation intending to do good and help—CAUTION: *Stop, listen and understand before helping.*

If you want to be an effective mentor, you need to have a solid understanding, not only of your protégés' school/professional lives, but their personal lives as well.

Having a holistic perspective is vital because your protégés' personal and school/professional lives intertwine and affect each other in various ways. It is impossible to separate their personal, family, or community concerns from their work or school concerns. Personal issues *will* creep into one's professional life. Or, school concerns might affect family issues. Even community and societal issues can be powerful forces in one's life.

Your protégé might not perform well at work because she is worried about her father's cancer. Another protégé might not be able to finish assignments because he is helping with the family business. Some protégés might fear going to school because the way to school is littered with drug paraphernalia and controlled by drug dealers.

Your protégé's life isn't conveniently compartmentalized into "work" or "school" in one pile and "personal life" in a separate pile. Hence, it is imperative that you understand the complexity of your protégés' lives, including their multiple roles and the contexts that are important to them—whether it is their church, synagogue, temple, mosque, extended family, school, college, workplace, community, clubs, friends, elders, or teachers. All these aspects come into play simultaneously as they try to navigate their school or professional lives.

If you want to be effective in helping your protégé succeed, you simply cannot ignore/dismiss/refuse to address "external" issues like the illness in the family, drug dealers in the neighborhood, or discrimination.

You can set a concrete foundation for your mentoring relationship by embracing, understanding and dealing with the complexity of your protégés' lives, their multiple identities, and the complicated mosaic of cultural values, history, family expectations, personal aspirations, community concerns, and societal pressures that affect and shape their experiences of the world.

PUTTING IT ALL TOGETHER—THE BIG PICTURE

All relationships are complex phenomena, and mentoring relationships are no exception. In the vast majority of mentoring relationships, differences occur in the form of gender, race, ethnicity, power, age, experience, generation, immigration status, family background, socioeconomic status, religion, and/or sexual orientation.

Although any one such difference can pose a challenge, these differences can be overcome and can even enrich and strengthen the relationship. The prerequisite for this to happen is each party's willingness to look at differences with honesty and openness and with utter regard, appreciation, and respect for each other. In particular, it is up to the mentor to be comfortable and competent in handling cultural differences.

A word of advice to potential mentors: it's not enough to want to make a difference. When reaching out to someone different from yourself, you need to have the skills and tools to navigate through obstacles along the way. You need to be able to earn your protégés' trust by being curious and by seeking to understand where they are coming from.

So, for instance, if your protégé is applying for a higher-level job and is worried about what this might mean in terms of family obligations, don't immediately dismiss these family concerns by saying "Your job comes first," or "Don't worry about your family—focus on yourself." Take a moment to reflect on these statements—do they reflect *your* values or your protégé's values?

You may value independence, achievement, and self-determination. These are all solid values dear to your heart, but these may not be values shared by your protégés. Instead, they may embrace values that are markedly different from your values, but are just as important, meaningful, and unshakeable to them.

A statement such as "focus on yourself" may dishonor your protégés' personal, cultural, and/or family values. A focus on the self may be completely contradictory to what they value. Instead, they may value heeding their family wishes over their own desires. Imagine if someone said a statement to you: "You are not important. Forget about yourself and focus on your family." See how jarring such a statement might be to you?

The best mentors are those who are open to understanding and dealing with the rich, sometimes surprising, sometimes conflicting set of cultural values, history, and beliefs that compose the worldviews of their protégés.

The pages ahead are your mentor's tool-kit as you embark on your cross-cultural mentoring journey. I encourage you to take a shot at the mentor practices described—each of these will contribute concretely to the success of your relationship in the three areas of relationship-building, developing your protégés' skills, and helping their professional and academic socialization.

But don't think of each practice in isolation—remember the big picture—the necessity to earn your protégés' trust, understand the complexity of their lives, and address relationship concerns. This big picture is the backdrop for the practical strategies showcased in this book.

Part I

Establishing the Mentoring Relationship and Building Trust

Career, professional, and academic support are often associated with mentoring. However, there is a lot more to mentoring than professional guidance.

Mentors need to earn their protégés' trust before they can enter into their lives and help them. In cross-racial relationships, it is all the more critical that trust is firmly established for a productive mentoring experience.

There are specific things you can do to establish a healthy, effective, and successful mentoring relationship. Each of these strategies will be discussed in-depth in the following chapters:

- giving time
- being available
- maintaining good communication
- keeping your word
- holistic understanding
- talking about race and culture
- listening
- providing emotional support
- telling about yourself
- acknowledging limitations
- acknowledging and repairing mistakes
- using humor
- giving gifts

Chapter 2

Giving Time

Time is the most valuable thing a man can spend.

—Laertius Diogenes (as cited in *Book of Positive Quotations*, 1993, pg. 273)

CASE EXAMPLE: A MENTOR GIVES TIME

Jesse came from a military family that moved every two or three years. On top of having to make new friends every other year, Jesse also had to deal with his dad being deployed overseas for long stretches of time. Jesse was close to his father and missed him desperately when he was gone. However, he bottled up his feelings. No one guessed that he was suffering inside.

Jesse might have gone under the radar indefinitely if not for Coach Isi, the physical education teacher at his junior high. Coach Isi noted that Jesse spent the longest day in school—his mom dropped him off before any other student so she could go to work. When school ended, Jesse went straight to the after-school program and his mom would pick him up at 7 pm.

Coach Isi invited Jesse to shoot hoops with him each morning before school started. Their early morning games became mentoring sessions on the basketball court where Jesse got to talk to Coach Isi about his feelings, hopes, fears, and dreams.

With each game, Coach Isi learned a little more about Jesse's life, including his father's deployment, his worries about his mother, and what it felt like to be a biracial African American/Filipino kid in a school that was predominantly white.

In exchange, Coach Isi told Jesse how he survived as the only Native American kid in an all-White school. His stories inspired Jesse and shored up his confidence that he too could survive.

The basketball court was not the only place where Coach Isi mentored students. His office door was always open, and he warmly welcomed anyone who popped in. His willingness to spend time was well known among the students, so much so that they affectionately called him "Counselor Coach."

Coach Isis's support and mentoring helped Jesse stay the course through the tough years of junior high. If you asked Coach Isi, he would say that he didn't do all that much other than shoot hoops with Jesse.

Jesse, however, would tell you a whole different version of what Coach Isi's time meant to him. "He spent just hours with me getting to know me, asking about my family, how it was growing up. He was very genuine and interested, and he shared of himself and was very real with me. More than any other teacher I've ever had, he knows all about my family life, my family problems, my everything. He knows me because he's bothered to ask. He cares to know. He's willing to put in the time. I just think that shows such a strong commitment."

WHY GIVING TIME MATTERS

Relationships are nourished and sustained by spending time together, whether through face-to-face meetings or phone contact. An essential ingredient to successful mentoring is spending time with your protégés—whether it is via e-mail, phone, or enjoying a soda together. When you give time to your protégés, you are sending a clear message that they matter to you, that their lives matter to you, and that you care enough to want to spend time with them.

In cross-cultural relationships, there might be an instinctive wariness and even mistrust at the beginning of the relationship when the protégé doesn't know the mentor well. One important way to build trust is to spend time with your protégés and get to know them, their hopes and dreams. It is also important for them to get to know you, your background, values, life history, experiences, and dreams. Only through mutual understanding can trust develop. And deep understanding can be achieved only when you take the time to be with your protégés.

I understand that people's lives are supercharged to the max and mentors might recoil at the thought of giving time to their protégés. However, even a quick phone-call or check-in means a lot. Don't forget that you can always enjoy a meal, play a game, or take a short walk with your protégé *and* spend quality, meaningful time with them.

PRACTICAL STRATEGIES FOR GIVING
AND SPENDING TIME WITH YOUR PROTÉGÉ

The message of this chapter is simple—be generous when giving time to your protégés, especially at the beginning of your relationship when you are getting to know each other. Spending time with your protégés sends a clear message that you care and like them enough to invest time in them.

Remember also that so-called "idle chitchat" serves an important function for bonding and trust-building.

Here are some simple Do's and Don'ts for spending time with your protégés:

- Do invite them to spend time with you. Think about how good it feels when someone wants to spend time with you! Be proactive in inviting your protégés to be with you. Don't wait for them to initiate action—you have to be the one to make the first move.
- Do give them as much time as they need, especially at the beginning of the relationship or when they are in distress.
- Don't rush when you are with them.
- Don't look at the time while they're talking.
- Don't restrict your availability to scheduled office hours.
- Do be absolutely present and attentive when you're with them.
- Don't multitask when you're with them (unless you are doing an activity together, like playing a sport).
- Try not to answer phone calls or text messages when you're with them.
- If they ask to talk to you at a bad time, explain your situation and offer alternatives to get together.
- If you have an office, keep your door open as much as possible to show your willingness to talk to your protégés.

Chapter 3

Being Available

So availability, I think, is a very important aspect . . . she was often in her room with the door open eithre working on a research project or talking to somebody. So that was something that was certainly a wonderful comfort and I think if she were not around as much it would have been difficult to develop that kind of rapport.

—Protégé (Chan, 2008, p. 269)

CASE EXAMPLE: WHAT ONE MENTOR'S AVAILABILITY MEANT TO HER PROTÉGÉ

After her tour of duty in Afghanistan, Sophia Jones returned home with a dream to establish a nonprofit organization to empower women vets with physical disabilities. Having suffered a head injury and a leg amputation, Sophia knew all too well the challenges of being a disabled vet in the civilian world.

Sophia's passion for her cause was undeniable. However, she initially got stymied by the numerous legal and logistic details of setting up a foundation. She had a million and one questions, but there was nobody in her life she could turn to. Left to her own devices, her dream might have died right there.

But she persisted in looking for help and chanced upon a local nonprofit support resource. When she visited the center for the first time, she immediately felt welcomed when a woman walking into the building held the door for her while she wheeled in. That encounter sparked a lively conversation about Sophia's hopes and dreams.

The woman who opened the door for Sophia was Laura Dominguez, the founder of the nonprofit support center.

Sophia found in Laura someone who believed in her and her dream. More importantly, she found someone who actively supported her dream.

Laura was someone who could answer her questions about board membership, fundraising, and all the nitty-gritty details of a nonprofit, such as "Who can be a board member?" and "What does "fictitious name" mean?"

Laura gave Sophia her work, cell, and home numbers, as well as her e-mail address. She made it clear that it was okay for Sophia to contact her. To Sophia's amazement, Laura actually answered her own phones and wrote her own e-mails. She did not have closed doors, stern secretaries, or rigid schedules barring Sophia from talking to her.

Sophia nervously called Laura on her cell when she had an issue that needed immediate guidance. Laura was at an out-of-state conference but she nevertheless warmly welcomed the call. They had a quick chat and Sophia got her question answered instantly.

Reflecting on the strength of her mentoring relationship, Sophia said: "As a person who gets around in a wheelchair, access is very important to me. But I'm not just talking about physical access. Laura opened the door for me literally as well as figuratively. She made herself accessible and available to me. Whenever I had a question, I could e-mail her or call her and she'd be there to answer. Her openness and availability was certainly a wonderful comfort. If she had been distant or rigid or was available only for an hour a week, it would have been difficult to develop that kind of rapport."

WHY BEING AVAILABLE MATTERS

How many of us have a direct line to someone important, say the president, the pope, or the CEO of Disneyland? I would imagine that few of us can pick up the phone, call someone like Oprah Winfrey, and say, "I need your advice on something. Can you help me?"

People in authority tend to be inaccessible to the average person. Multiple barriers are intentionally set up to protect them from outsiders.

What sets mentors apart is their willingness to be accessible and available. A mentor's availability is enormously comforting to a protégé. It means that there is someone to turn to for an answer. It also sends a clear message that the protégé matters.

Having access to someone within the organization is enormously helpful in making a newcomer feel welcomed. For ethnic minorities in particular, entering a new environment can be intimidating and overwhelming, especially if the environment is not overtly friendly to minorities. A mentor's open door (both literally and figuratively) goes a long way in making them feel like they belong and are welcomed. Often, the mentor serves as the one crucial link between the student/employee and the organization.

Lest potential mentors panic at the thought of protégés pounding constantly at their door, I should point out that most protégés are extremely respectful and appreciative of their mentors' time because they recognize that the mentor's availability is a rare gift.

Should a protégé step out of line, the mentor can turn the misstep into a learning opportunity to discuss the meaning and limits of the mentor's availability.

PRACTICAL STRATEGIES FOR BEING AVAILABLE TO YOUR PROTÉGÉS

- Discuss with your protégés their needs for communication and your wish to be available to them.
- Ask about their preferred mode of communication. A young protégé might prefer texting, while others may prefer regular face-to-face contact.
- Be available to your protégés as much as possible. If possible, give them multiple ways to get a hold of you. Tell them you welcome their calls and e-mails. You can adjust this based on your own comfort level and need for privacy. Some mentors might prefer not to give home numbers, but could provide other ways to be contacted in case of emergencies.
- Be prompt in responding to calls and e-mails. Don't keep them waiting for long periods of time.
- Keep your door open—literally and metaphorically.
- Tell them when you won't be available and give them alternate numbers or people to call during that time.
- If you are going to be unavailable, leave an automatic e-mail reply or phone message stating when you will return and other means to get in touch with you.

Chapter 4

Maintaining Good Communication

After all, when you come right down to it, how many people speak the same language even when they speak the same language?

—Russell Hoban (as cited in *The Merriam-Webster Dictionary of Quotations,* 1992, p. 64)

CASE EXAMPLE: A MENTOR'S GREAT COMMUNICATION EARNS HIS PROTÉGÉ'S TRUST

Growing up in a tough neighborhood in Atlanta, Hussein had been considered an "at risk" kid. But thanks to his dedicated mom and a caring community who watched closely over him, he succeeded even with the odds stacked against him. Turning down full scholarships from Yale and Princeton, he opted to go to a historically Black college where he received a top-notch education in a place that honored and enriched his identity as an African American.

After graduating summa cum laude, he decided to stretch his wings. He made the tough decision to leave his beloved community in Atlanta and accepted a job offer at a major firm in the East Coast.

The Nor'easter wasn't the only chill that blasted him when he arrived. The top management acted like an exclusive club—no one took the time to welcome him or reach out to him. He felt doubly isolated as the only Black professional in the entire company.

He made many attempts to get to know his colleagues and managers, but wasn't sure how to respond to subtly racist remarks, such as compliments about him not being like "other Black folks."

17

To rub salt in the wound, Hussein woke up one day to discover that someone had burnt a cross in his front lawn when he was on a weekend vacation.

Another time, the mosque where he attended was egged and defaced with hate messages such as "Go home Osama."

Hussein became increasingly suspicious, distrustful, and stressed. New to the area, he did not know whom to turn to or trust.

Just as he was contemplating moving back to Atlanta, the firm shifted operations and Hussein was placed under the supervision of the second-in-command at the company. Jack Jones, an Irish American, had painstakingly worked his way up the career ladder, starting as a chauffeur for the CEO. Jack knew what it was like to be excluded from the insiders' circle and made a special effort to get to know Hussein.

At first, Hussein did not trust Jack. He had been burnt one too many times. "How is he different from other White people?" was his initial thought.

Jack proved to be not only an exceptional manager, but an exceptional mentor as well. For starters, he took pains to get to know Hussein, his culture, and his family. He was genuinely interested in Hussein's religion and even visited his mosque with him. He was willing to listen to Hussein's painful experiences. Much to Hussein's surprise, he acknowledged that racism exists and that the system privileged one group over others.

Jack also earned Hussein's trust by being absolutely responsive in communicating. He floored Hussein with his dependability and responsiveness. When Jack said he'd call, he did. When Hussein wrote an e-mail to Jack, he responded right away. If Hussein left a message for Jack, Jack would return the call within minutes (on a work day) or hours (if he was out of town).

Not once did Jack ignore Hussein's voice messages or e-mails.

Said Hussein about Jack's responsiveness: "I think it's really important because I have lots of questions a lot of the time and I don't always have time to meet with him and there aren't really that many times where we both have an hour free. If he weren't responsive, I would get really frustrated because I like a lot of feedback, and I like bouncing ideas off of people. I've had bosses who weren't responsive, and I would be constantly waiting for a response. They made me feel frustrated and insignificant. Jack's level of responsiveness shows that he understands the value of mentorship and that I can count on him."

WHY GOOD COMMUNICATION AND
MENTOR RESPONSIVENESS MATTER

All the protégés in my research studies emphasized the importance of their mentors' responsiveness. Curious as to exactly how responsive these mentors were, I calculated the amount of time they took to reply to their protégés' e-mails that were sent during business hours (I excluded e-mails that contained requests for lengthy feedback). Astonishingly, the mentors answered their protégés' e-mails in an average of 2.7 hours!

One of the key pieces in building trust in a relationship is establishing good communication. This is particularly crucial when cross-racial and cross-cultural differences are involved. When cultural mistrust is present, mentors can do a lot to ease tension and earn trust by being responsive. Responding quickly to an e-mail or phone call may sound trivial but it sends an important message that you care and that your protégés matter to you.

PRACTICAL STRATEGIES FOR MAINTAINING GOOD COMMUNICATION

- Be prompt in responding to your protégés' phone calls and e-mails. As far as possible, respond as soon as you can. Try not to delay or keep them waiting.
- Apologize if you are not able to respond in a timely manner.
- If you are unable to respond promptly, inform your protégé beforehand. Set up an automatic e-mail/voicemail response for the period when you will not be able to respond.
- If possible, tell your protégés when you will be away from e-mail/calls and give them ways to contact you when you are not available.
- Be proactive in communicating with your protégé. Take the initiative to make a phone call or send an e-mail, text message, letter, or card to ask, "How are you doing?" A simple check-in once in a while tells them you care and are thinking of them.
- Be aware of cultural differences in communicating and adjust your style accordingly—some Asians prefer less eye contact. Some cultures are more touchy-feely, while others prefer respect for personal space. Some cultures are very direct when communicating, whereas other groups prefer indirect or story-telling approach. Some younger people and introverts might prefer technology over face-to-face interactions.

Chapter 5

Keeping Your Word

We judge ourselves by what we feel capable of doing, while others judge us by what we have already done.

—Henry Wadsworth Longfellow (as cited in *The Giant Book of American Quotations*, 1988, p. 125)

CASE EXAMPLE: MENTORS WHO TALK THE TALK AND WALK THE WALK

Jose grew up in circumstances that few could imagine. His father disappeared before he was born. His mother was addicted to crack before, during, and after his birth. Jose spent the first five years of his life in the chaotic environment of a crack house.

Unpredictability was the norm in Jose's experience of his mom and her friends. There was no such thing as a "meal" in his home—food appeared whenever someone thought to get some. No one was able or willing to deliver on the simplest promise. Nobody's word was good.

On one of her rare lucid mornings, his mom promised to take him to the mall to get him a toy. But an hour later, some friends dropped by with a stash of crack. They started doing drugs, and she was high the rest of the day. They didn't go to the mall, and Jose didn't get the toy she promised.

Not surprisingly, Jose learned not to count on anyone.

Jose's life took a dramatic turn when he started kindergarten. His teachers suspected he was being abused and contacted Social Services.

Jose was immediately placed in a foster home. His foster mom and dad were kind, steady folks who were as different as could be from the people Jose was used to. When his foster parents told him they would pick him up from school, they were there as promised. When they said they'd take him to Little League, they did so. When they said they were going to take him to buy shoes, they followed through and Jose relished the feel of his first ever new pair of shoes.

Another anchor and mentor for Jose was his kindergarten teacher Roberto—a deeply caring soul who poured his heart into his life mission to educate young people from impoverished homes. He was the kind of teacher who visited every single student at home and took the time to get to know each student's family.

Jose and Roberto connected over their love for baseball and spent hours at recess talking about their favorite baseball team. Roberto told him he'd loan him a book about baseball greats. Sure enough, as promised, Roberto brought the book the next day.

At first, Jose was unsure and suspicious about the new strangers in his life. He was completely unused to being around people who kept their word.

But their repeated and persistent demonstrations of consistency and reliability slowly undid Jose's skepticism. He made a big transition in his heart—he began to love and trust.

After a year of recuperation from his rough start in life, he blossomed. His transformation was nothing short of a miracle—he went from being a frightened, distrustful child to one who was able to give and accept love.

WHY KEEPING YOUR WORD MATTERS

It seems so simple—doing what one says one is going to do.

But how many people in your life are dependable and stay true to their word? How many times have people said, "I'll call you!" but that's the last you hear from them?

If you say to a protégé, "I'll call you," then be sure to do so.

If you say you're going to help with a project, then show up and give the help you promised.

If you say you're going to give your protégé something, then be sure to follow through and make good on your promise.

If you offer to connect your protégé with a colleague, make that connection.

If you are going to meet at a specific time, show up on time.

You might ask, "What's so bad about a little slip-up now and then—we're all human, right?"

The answer is simple, and I'll phrase it in the form of a question—would *you* trust and count on someone who is unreliable? Would you listen to the advice of someone who talks the talk but doesn't walk the walk?

Of course people are human and slip-ups, mistakes, and lapses do happen. Should you let your protégé down, be sure to model the best of human behavior when you are less than your best self: apologize directly, acknowledge your mistake, and if necessary, make amends. Don't make excuses, deny the facts, change the subject, or blame your protégé—these are all sure-fire ways to damage your relationship and alienate your protégé.

But let your slip-ups be the rare occurrence rather than the norm. Repeated letdowns, even little ones, are like acid on metal. They slowly but surely erode the foundation of trust and respect in a relationship. When a relationship is in the beginning stages, these letdowns are especially corrosive to the burgeoning trust that is struggling to take root.

Remember that trust isn't automatically created at the beginning of a relationship. In cross-racial relationships, you cannot assume that your protégés will trust you instantly just because you have good intentions to help them.

A mentor has to *earn* a protégé's trust. One of the key ways to earn someone's trust is by being good to your word.

If you want to be an outstanding mentor, *be* outstanding in your dependability, reliability, and your word. Do what you say. Keep your promises. It's really as simple as that.

PRACTICAL STRATEGIES FOR KEEPING YOUR WORD

- The formula for would-be mentors *is* simple—don't promise what you can't deliver. Or to put it in positive terms—do what you say you're going to do.
- Ask yourself: "Do my words line up with my actions?" and "Do I deliver on my promises?"
- Reflect on the last time you failed to keep your word. Ask yourself: "Did I handle my slip-up in a constructive or destructive way?" and "How might this experience serve as a teaching moment for me and my protégé?"
- If you slip up, acknowledge your mistake, apologize, and make up for your mistake. Don't deny your slip-up, make excuses, or blame your protégé. Be a role model for how to handle slip-ups.

Chapter 6

Holistic Understanding

There is a great difference between knowing a thing and understanding it.

—Charles Kettering with T. A. Boyd (as cited in *"Quotable" Quotes: Wit and Wisdom for Every Occasion,* 1997, p. 25)

CASE STUDY: HOW ONE MENTOR'S HOLISTIC UNDERSTANDING HELPED HER PROTÉGÉ'S CAREER

Two middle-aged women are at a little hole-in-a-wall restaurant noshing on *chaat* (Indian snacks) downed with mango *lassi* (a yogurt drink). They laugh and chat nonstop as they dive into their food and their lives. At first glance, the pair appear to be two friends catching up on each other's lives as they range over topics such as families, children, and careers. But pay closer attention and you will witness real mentoring going on, inseparable from the chatter about personal lives.

The two met when Sonica, a first-generation South Asian American woman, volunteered at a community hospital where Dr. Rashida, an African American woman, worked as an internist.

With their shared passion for good food and medicine, they bonded fast as they got to know each other by exchanging stories of their lives. Although they came from vastly different racial and cultural backgrounds, they developed a solid mentoring relationship anchored in a foundation of deep understanding and respect for each other's family, community, and multiple identities.

Rashida never expressed displeasure or discomfort when Sonica brought up topics that were not directly career-related. Not once did Rashida say to Sonica, "Let's just focus on your work issues. Home stuff is not relevant to mentoring."

25

Instead, she understood that work is not divorced from other parts of an individual's life. So she listened, with interest and patience, when Sonica told stories about her family, husband, son, and in-laws. She recognized these were interlocking parts of Sonica's life that shaped and enhanced who she was as a professional.

Said Sonica: "She would ask me about my life, like 'How's your family?' And so she would very much connect on a personal level and not shy away from that. She would be genuinely interested."

Rashida herself freely brought up topics that were not strictly work-related, like how she balanced work with taking care of her large extended family and her ailing father, and what it meant to be a highly successful, professional single woman in her culture.

Rashida's ease with discussing life issues reassured Sonica that Rashida understood what it was like to cope with personal challenges. Sonica grew to trust Rashida's guidance because she knew that Rashida had a thorough understanding of the complexity of her situation.

With Rashida's guidance, Sonica made it through med school, even with twin babies on the way. After med school, Sonica felt conflicted about applying for residencies that would take her away from her newborn babies for many hours. She knew what was truly important to her when she experienced relief, rather than disappointment, when she was turned down for a residency.

Luckily, Rashida understood how important family life was to Sonica. Over many meals at different restaurants, they mapped out an alternative plan that would enable Sonica to be in the healthcare field without the intensive training demands required of a doctor.

Sonica applied to an accelerated nursing program that accepted most of the coursework she had already completed. She became a nurse practitioner, allowing her to have the patient contact she loved, work in the medical field, *and* have sufficient family time.

Said Sonica: "We're not just talking about work when we meet . . . family is important to me and to her and so we share that. When I feel that somebody knows what I'm dealing with in my life, both academic and clinical work, I feel understood because what's been hard for me is keeping up with my family responsibilities. I needed somebody to know that was a big piece and I couldn't avoid that. I felt she got it and she would encourage me to not get weighed down by things. I'm not sure other people would have wanted to hear all of that. For me, that was really important."

To this day, she and Rashida continue to meet once a week at a local restaurant. Their weekly mentoring dinner is the one constant in the midst of their constantly evolving careers and lives.

WHY HAVING A HOLISTIC UNDERSTANDING MATTERS

Having a holistic understanding of your protégés means having a full understanding of their families, cultures, communities, and lives beyond work or school. This understanding is crucial for knowing who your protégés are, what makes them tick, what their strengths and support systems are, and what might derail their progress.

Your protégés belong in multiple worlds of school/work, family, religious organizations, communities, and society at large. These worlds influence and shape them in various ways . . . and can sometimes collide. If you focus solely on your protégés' school or work issues, you are missing big parts of who they are and the challenges they face. You can be so much more effective and powerful as a mentor if you embrace their multiple identities and seek to understand the different environments they swim in.

One protégé I interviewed stated emphatically, "If you get the cultural piece, you get the layer. You get the middle contextual layer about a person that shapes how they think, how they dream, how they work, how they prioritize things in their life. . . . For a mentor not to understand that, then it's meaningless."

Be curious about the complexity of your protégé's life. Get to know your protégés by initiating questions about their lives and the people in their lives. Showing interest in their lives tells them that you care.

At the same time, watch for the very human tendency to think and judge in terms of stereotypes. Question your assumptions about different races. Even a seemingly positive stereotype such as the "model minority myth" or a statement like "you Asians are all good in math," can be harmful in pigeon-holing Asian Americans.

It might take a while for your protégés to trust you and open up to you. Just be patient. The efforts you invest in getting to know your protégés—to know about all the different parts of their lives—will pay off for them as well as for your mentoring relationships.

PRACTICAL STRATEGIES FOR HAVING A HOLISTIC UNDERSTANDING

Use the following strategies to help increase your understanding of your protégé and build closeness and trust in your relationship.

Take the lead from your protégé—be sensitive to how they respond when you first ask them about themselves. Back off if your protégé is not ready to disclose at a particular moment. Remember that earning trust takes time. You don't have to be invasive or push your protégé to open up.

- Ask yourself: what are the key components that might affect your protégé's life? Refer to the Checklist Table 6.1, pg. 29 to identify important facets of your protégé's identity. Be curious when your protégé refers to any of these pieces. Ask them to tell you more.
- Tell them you are interested in their lives.
- Be proactive in asking questions—don't wait for them to open up. See the section below for sample questions.
- Ask what their journeys and aspirations mean to those closest to them, such as their children, parents, extended families, partners, cultural, and spiritual communities.
- Ask about family and community obligations and how these obligations enrich and/or detract from their goals.
- Try this exercise with children and teens: give them a piece of paper with a series of five concentric circles. Have them write their names in the inner-most circle. Ask them to write the names of the people they are closest to in the circle next to their name. Have them write the names of other people within the circles, according to degrees of closeness. Discuss with them what it means that someone is within or not within their inner circle.
- Show genuine interest by listening and asking more questions when they talk about themselves, their personal lives, and the important people in their lives.
- Question your assumptions and stereotypes about other groups.
- Don't assume you understand the lived experience of the other person's life experiences and culture.
- Sometimes a conversation about work or school may veer off into another direction if personal issues come up. Stay present with your protégé. It's okay to have an occasional detour.
- Talk about your own identities and how these have affected your life.

QUESTIONS TO GET YOU STARTED TOWARD A HOLISTIC UNDERSTANDING OF YOUR PROTÉGÉ

- "How is your family doing?"
- "Who are your good friends at school or work?"
- "Who are people you look up to?"
- "Tell me about your brothers and sisters. What are they like?"
- "Who are the most important people in your life and how do they influence your goals?"
- "What kinds of family or community responsibilities do you have?"

- "What are activities that you enjoy outside school or work?"
- "What's it like to be a (fill in with detail about your protégé's life, e.g. only child, 2nd-generation Asian American, etc.)?"
- "What's your family's history? What events led to you being here at this point in time?"
- "What are your parents'/partners'/children's dreams for you?"

Table 6.1. Checklist of Key Components of an Individual's Identity and Life

Reflect on which of the following apply to your protégés. Pay attention when they refer to these parts of their identities. Ask questions and be curious about these aspects of lives.

In addition, think about how you differ from your protégés in any of these areas. Ask yourself and your protégés how these differences might affect communication and understanding between you and them.

- gender
- personal history, life story, life circumstances
- sexual orientation
- age
- generation
- educational level
- religion
- spirituality
- race
- ethnicity
- immigration history
- level of acculturation and parents' level of acculturation
- family and extended family history
- family type (e.g., nuclear, extended, single parent, etc.)
- family values and expectations
- family obligations and responsibilities
- socioeconomic status
- national origin
- geographical origin
- marital status
- birth order
- abilities and disabilities
- political beliefs
- health conditions
- language abilities
- veteran status
- beliefs about power, hierarchy, authority, and position in society

Chapter 7

Talking about Race and Culture

But race is an issue that I believe this nation cannot afford to ignore right now. . . . The fact is that the comments that have been made and the issues that have surfaced over the last few weeks reflect the complexities of race in this country that we've never really worked through—a part of our union that we have yet to perfect. And if we walk away now, if we simply retreat into our respective corners, we will never be able to come together and solve challenges like health care, or education, or the need to find good jobs for every American. . . . But I have asserted a firm conviction—a conviction rooted in my faith in God and my faith in the American people—that working together we can move beyond some of our old racial wounds, and that in fact we have no choice if we are to continue on the path of a more perfect union.

—Senator Barack Obama, speech in Philadelphia, Pennsylvania,
(March 18, 2008)

CASE EXAMPLE OF TALKING ABOUT RACE AND CULTURE: A PERSONAL EXAMPLE

Someone once said to me, "Anne—I don't see you as Asian. I just see you like any other person." I was both dumbfounded and saddened by this statement, well-meaning as it undoubtedly was. If this individual doesn't see me as Asian, then how am I to talk about the parts of myself that have to do with my Chinese heritage? How would it be possible for us to have a relationship if he doesn't see me as an Asian woman and a person of color?

I have friendships that have been less than satisfying because I have not been able to be fully me — by this I mean I have not been able to talk fully and openly about myself as a Chinese woman, a person of color, an immigrant, someone who has experienced painful racist, sexist, and other discriminatory experiences.

Conversely, I have been extremely fortunate in being able to enjoy relationships where we each had a deep understanding of each other's cultures and identities. This understanding has enabled both parties to know, appreciate, and acknowledge each other's totality of experience, personal history, challenges, and triumphs.

One such person in my life is Joe. Right from the get-go, Joe made the effort to ask me about my background and my family history. Early on in our relationship, he quickly got to know the big headlines of my life—that I had come to the United States all by myself when I was eighteen, that I had landed in Berkeley without any idea what Berkeley was all about, that I had no biological family in the United States.

He himself was open about himself and his experiences as a Black man. There was never any question that he identified as a Black man. He was direct and unapologetic about his race and the way race has played out in his life. He didn't skirt or avoid the topic, but was at ease discussing or referring to his race, just as he might his wife, daughters, and career journey.

Joe's openness about his race and racial identity encouraged me to be similarly open.

We freely discussed his experiences in the Civil Rights Movement, his experiences with racism, his struggles with unjust systems. We never had to skirt issues of race—we were both solidly grounded in an understanding and appreciation of each other's race, culture, and identity.

I appreciated this openness for multiple reasons. First, I could be myself— I didn't have to hide parts of myself or avoid talking about pieces of myself that were important to me. Second, I could understand Joe more fully—I have few relationships with older Black men, and it was a privilege for me to know him at a deeper level. Third, I appreciate the ease with which I can talk about race and racism—there's no awkwardness, no fear of offense, dismissal, rejection, or of being shut down. When discriminatory events happened, I could turn safely to him and feel assured that I could get understanding and support from him.

Talking about race and culture has helped Joe get a deeper understanding of where I'm coming from and the unique challenges faced by me as a result of my culture, gender, race, life experiences, and upbringing. For instance, one of my big struggles is speaking up and being assertive. In working with me on this issue, Joe has been sensitive to the multiple factors hindering my progress in this area. In one e-mail, he wrote:

Hi Anne, In terms of culture, gender and family, you were taught to keep your head down, be extremely modest and hide in the corner. You now live in America where if you want to have a voice, you have to find a way that is culturally and gender congruent to speak and be heard without becoming narcissistic, arrogant or boasting. I think you're slowly finding your way and it all looks good.

Keep the faith, Joe.

Imagine for a moment that Joe and I did not talk about race or culture. Imagine that these topics are off-limits or that Joe was uncomfortable talking about race and culture. The effect of this restriction would mean that at the very least our conversations would be severely limited. Many topics would at best lack depth and at worst, would be off limits. Joe would not fully understand why I have such difficulties being assertive. I might be frustrated by my lack of progress and my inability to communicate why I am facing such difficulty. I'd likely feel misunderstood by Joe. Deleted would be the camaraderie, understanding, and appreciation gleaned from the sharing of each other's life experiences and views.

WHY TALKING ABOUT RACE AND CULTURE MATTERS

There's a great story about the elephant in the living room—everyone knows about it, yet no one talks about it. Any sensitive topic—whether it's an issue of race, culture, sexual orientation, discrimination—is the elephant in the living room.

We skirt it, avoid it, change the subject—even though it's definitely there and it's huge. We're afraid to address it, and so we keep avoiding the topic. We pretend not to notice while the elephant stays in the living room, trampling on precious family heirlooms, damaging everything and everybody in its way.

In many relationships there's often a code of silence around sensitive topics. These taboo topics are not up for discussion. But the elephant is definitely in the room.

Of course, talking openly, frankly, and meaningfully about issues of race, culture, racism, injustice, inequality, and discrimination can be discomforting and difficult. This is particularly true between two people who are from different racial and/or cultural groups and who have unequal power status.

However, the ability to talk about race can have serious implications for a protégé's career. One Harvard researcher (Thomas, 2001) found that minorities tend to advance further when their White mentors acknowledged and understood the impact of race on their protégés.

Moreover, talking about race and culture can result in a number of positive benefits for mentoring relationships, including:

* facilitating a deeper understanding of each other
* fostering rapport
* enhancing trust
* building ease and comfort
* helping the protégé feel understood

PRACTICAL STRATEGIES FOR TALKING ABOUT RACE

In relationships with cross-cultural differences, remember that it takes time to develop trust. Be patient with the development of the relationship. You simply cannot expect that your protégé will trust you instantly when they do not know you.

Understand what *your* fears and insecurities are when it comes to talking about race and discrimination (see Table 7.1). Few people would think of asking someone: "What it is it like to be in your shoes as a Black man in America?" or "What was your experience as an immigrant to this country?" These questions can trigger a lot of anxiety for both mentors and protégé. Some may fear that the other gets offended by the question. They may fear they are prying; or they are worried about using the word "Black." Some hesitate because they don't know which is the "right" word to use—"Black" or "African American." Some fear bringing up the race issue might trigger a discussion they can't handle.

However, it is only by asking these questions and being honest about who you are and what you know or don't know that you can genuinely connect with someone different from yourself.

Likewise, not everyone (even those from minority groups) feels comfortable talking about race or racial issues. However, it's important that you as the mentor demonstrate your sensitivity, interest, and competency in handling racial and cultural issues. Unexpected situations involving all kinds of cultural variables can and do pop up, and it is vital that you as the mentor are comfortable and skillful in addressing these issues with your protégé.

These are basic strategies for becoming knowledgeable and comfortable in talking about uncomfortable topics:

* Examine your discomfort around sensitive topics (see Table 7.1). Take steps to enlarge your comfort zone.
* Show your interest by asking questions about your protégé's many cultural identities, be it gender, race, or sexual orientation. For example, ask what it

means to be a member of a minority group. Ask questions and listen with interest and openness.

- Seek consultation from others about sensitive topics, for example, the proper term to use or the correct etiquette.
- Be honest and open about what you know and don't know about a person's culture, and be open about your lack of knowledge as well as your eagerness to learn.
- Be open to listening to your protégés' stories about their personal lives, even if these stories are difficult for you to hear—these stories are the gateway for you to enter their world and their culture.
- Seek to understand and learn, rather than to argue and debate.
- Discussing race or culture does not always have to be serious or heavy handed. One can indirectly engage these topics through discussions of food, family, movies, cultural traditions, or books.
- Increase your knowledge about other cultures. Good ways to get started include reading, talking to people, and attending cultural events.

Table 7.1. Obstacles to Listening and Talking about Race

When someone pushes racism into my awareness, I feel guilty (that I could be doing so much more), angry (I don't like to feel like I'm wrong), defensive (I already have two Black friends . . . I worry more about racism than most Whites do—isn't that enough), turned off (I have other priorities in my life—with guilt about that thought), helpless (the problem is so big—what can I do?). *I hate to feel this way.* That is why I minimize race issues and let them fade from my awareness whenever possible (Winter, 1977, p. 24).

Winter lists a number of defenses that causes her to minimize race issues. What are your obstacles to listening and talking about race and culture? How can you overcome these obstacles?

Put an "X" if this is true of you	My Obstacles to Listening & Talking Openly about Race and Culture	How I can Overcome my Obstacles
	Anger	
	Not believing the legitimacy of topic	
	Not believing the importance of topic	
	Fear	
	Defensiveness	
	Guilt	
	Helplessness	
	Impatience	
	Discomfort	
	Uncertainty	
	Lack of knowledge	
	Other: _____	

Chapter 8

Listening

The greatest gift you can give another is the purity of your attention.

—Richard Moss, MD (as cited in *"Quotable" Quotes: Wit and Wisdom for Every Occasion,* 1997, p. 124)

CASE EXAMPLE: A MENTOR LISTENS . . . AND MAKES A DIFFERENCE

Silei was a quiet Samoan pre-teen from a lively family comprising ten brothers and sisters. Her family's house was a constant hub of activity with an ever-present, ever-changing constellation of siblings, cousins, and friends. There was always someone in the house to play or hang out with, so boredom was never an issue.

The only downside to being part of a big family was that Silei never had alone time with either parent. Mom and Dad were in constant motion, working, doing household chores, or attending to one child or another.

A caring teacher thought a mentor would be helpful for Silei. He told her parents about a local Big Sisters program and helped Silei with the application. Silei was paired with Mary, a sophomore from a nearby community college. At first glance, they appeared to be polar opposites—Mary came from a traditional New England family and was the only child of older parents. Despite these differences, they took a quick liking to each other, bonding over their love for ethnic food, Harry Potter, and running marathons.

Mary was a generous soul who loved giving Silei inexpensive gifts such as nail polish and trinkets. But Mary's greatest gift was her ability and willingness to listen. She was interested in all of Silei's stories—what it was like to immigrate, her first impressions of America, her struggles in school as an ESL student, her joys and triumphs, and experiences growing up in a big family.

Mary listened with patience and with presence. She expressed interest and asked appropriate questions whenever Silei wanted to share a story. She gave input and made suggestions only after she had listened carefully and received a clear picture of what was going on.

Mary never interrupted when Silei spoke. Nor did she answer her cell phone, text, or multi-task. Even if they were in a crowd of people she would maintain good eye contact and be focused on Silei.

At first, Silei was taken aback that Mary was interested in her life. Silei didn't think her life was all that interesting, plus no one had ever given her this much one-on-one attention. Over time, Mary's attentiveness became the key to winning Silei's trust. Mary's demonstrated interest prompted Silei to be comfortable confiding in her, thus enabling Mary to offer guidance, support, and advice as needed.

"She's such a great listener," said Silei shyly when I asked her what she liked about Mary. It was a simple statement, but it conveyed the essence of what Mary meant to her.

WHY LISTENING MATTERS

Listening is one of the pillars of mentoring. Without careful listening, mentoring simply cannot take place.

There is tremendous power in the simple act of listening. Taking the time to listen tells your protégés that you care, that you are interested, and that you value them.

Yet, the ability to listen is often underrated and overlooked. Think about it—during the course of a day, how many times do you feel completely listened to?

One way to learn how to be a better listener is to pay attention to how many people make the effort to listen. Often, people are so quick to interrupt with their stories, talk about themselves, offer advice, or propose solutions that they don't even hear the person they are with.

The result is countless numbers of missed opportunities to listen and to make someone feel heard and understood.

Pay attention to the ways in which people disengage from listening—learn from these mistakes to improve your own listening skills.

Be attentive to your protégé. Even if you are an online mentor, pay attention to what they are saying (or typing) and be responsive.

Ask and listen to your protégés' stories about their race and culture. We seldom ask about other people's cultural experiences because we are too embarrassed or too afraid to inquire. However, these stories form the backbone of your protégé's life, outlook, and beliefs. Listening to these stories, even if it pains you, will pay off in huge dividends for your relationship.

PRACTICAL STRATEGIES FOR GOOD LISTENING

- Practice good listening skills—maintain good eye contact, stay focused on what your protégé is saying, and don't do other tasks while your protégé is speaking to you. (Note, however, that some people, cultures, and age groups prefer less, rather than more eye contact.)
- Turn off any distractions, for example, Blackberries, cell phones, computers. Don't pick up the phone in the middle of your conversation with your protégé. If you absolutely *have* to take a call when you're with a protégé, explain why the call is important to you.
- Watch and curb any tendency toward formulating a response while you are listening. Try to listen, just listen.
- *Always* listen first, before giving input, feedback, advice, or suggestions.
- Know that it's perfectly okay to *not* have a response immediately.
- Ask clarifying questions to make sure you are getting what your protégé is saying, for example, "Am I hearing you correctly that. . . ."
- Recap what your protégé is saying to let them know you understand. "Let me see if I'm getting what you saying _____."
- The venue for listening can be vital. Make sure your protégé has privacy to talk. An ideal place is a quiet space without distractions and interruptions, away from nosy peers or colleagues. For older protégés, going to a café can be helpful.
- It is generally best not to multi-task when having a serious conversation. However, for some younger children and young adults, doing an activity together can facilitate the conversation. Activities that are conducive to conversation include coloring, doing a puzzle, modeling clay, going for a walk, and shooting hoops. Some kids may prefer to hold onto a toy or stuffed animal when they are talking. Others may be more open to talking when they are moving around.

Chapter 9

Providing Emotional Support

In order to be a mentor and an effective one, one must care. You must care. You don't have to know how many square miles are in Idaho, you don't need to know what is the chemical makeup of chemistry, or of blood or water. Know what you know and care about the person, care about what you know and care about the person you're sharing with.

—Maya Angelou (2008)

CASE EXAMPLE: A MALE MENTOR PROVIDES EMOTIONAL SUPPORT FOR A FEMALE PROTÉGÉ

Rosario was a rarity in the engineering world—a woman and a Latina with advanced degrees in engineering and business. With her winning combination of intelligence, technical know-how, and charisma, she shot up the corporate ladder, enjoying rapid promotions from engineer to project leader, and then to senior management.

Her meteoric rise stopped abruptly when she became pregnant with her first child and took maternity leave for a year—her first sabbatical from a paid job since she was fifteen.

All at once, she was thrust into a chaotic world of new motherhood with a special needs child who slept little and cried a lot. Nothing in the business world had prepared her for this experience. She had always been successful as a student and professional, but felt thoroughly overwhelmed by the demands of motherhood.

When her baby was at his most colicky, inconsolable self, Rosario felt
she would go stark howling mad. In the pit of sleep-deprived despair, she
e-mailed her mentor late one night, desperate for some comfort.

Here is her mentor's response, reassuring Rosario that her world would
find its center in due course:

> Hi Rosario, You are entirely right. Your world has shrunk, big time. In time
> it will gradually redefine itself and new balances will be established. I guar-
> antee you that life will take on a new calmness, and you will get some sleep
> eventually.
>
> There's not much existential thinking to do in the early stages of parent-
> hood. The mode is just one of survival until things begin to clear a little bit. So
> just hang in there and don't worry about the outside world too much for right
> now. The outside world isn't going anywhere and it will be there when you get
> ready for it again.
>
> Stay strong!
>
> Bob

Rosario's mentor was right, of course. In time, Rosario found her stride balancing her mom and manager roles. As she acclimated to her new reality, Bob was
solidly by her side, offering sympathy, reassurance, and advice when needed.

Note that Rosario's mentor was a man who had never experienced motherhood. However, he was genuinely interested in Rosario's experiences—he
didn't made assumptions, but instead asked lots of questions to gain a real
understanding of what she was going through. He listened patiently and was
sympathetic whenever Rosario shared her struggles.

Another way he supported her was by introducing Rosario to a woman a
few years her senior who was also a mom and a manager. The two bonded
instantly, trading survival tips such as how to get to work on time and how to
pump milk at work. This woman understood exactly what Rosario was going
through and was another vital source of support for her.

Rosario credits her mentor for helping her integrate her identities of mother
and worker. Without his genuine caring and support, she believes she might
not have persisted in finding a way to balance the oftentimes conflicting roles
of mom and manager.

WHY PROVIDING EMOTIONAL SUPPORT MATTERS

The long journey toward a career goal is never smooth. Along the way, your
protégé is likely to encounter bumps and potholes that will hinder, delay, or
even derail progress. Whenever your protégé hits a snag, it is enormously

comforting and helpful if you are there to reassure, extend a helping hand, and serve as a safety net of kindness, understanding, and warmth.

Some mentors might shy away from asking about protégés' personal challenges and lives. However, since personal issues can affect work or school performance, it's important that mentors have a working knowledge of what's going on in a protégé's life beyond school or work. This is especially important when you are mentoring someone culturally different from yourself. Without this understanding, you might offer limited or even inappropriate guidance based on a one dimensional view of your protégé's life.

Talking about personal struggles can be a big benefit to the protégé. Having the support of a mentor helps the protégé gain perspective, learn from the mentor's experiences, and rebound faster.

This is not to say that a mentor should act as a counselor or psychotherapist. It's perfectly okay to be supportive and offer guidance if the protégé has a problem that can be resolved fairly straightforwardly. If the problem is ongoing, protracted, and needs more long-term intensive help and support, then it is probable that the protégé would need professional help beyond what a mentor can offer.

You can refer your protégé to specialists, such as psychotherapists and psychologists, but the timing of making the referral has to be right.

One seasoned mentor cautioned that mentors should not immediately shut protégés down or refer them to someone else when they bring up personal issues: "Opening up to you means they trust you. You can't say: "No, no, no, don't tell me that. I don't want to hear that. That isn't the mentor's job." You have to be careful because you don't want to reject the person, or it's going to be a long time before they open up to somebody else. Shutting them down may also damage your mentoring relationship."

PRACTICAL STRATEGIES FOR BEING EMOTIONALLY SUPPORTIVE

Offering emotional support means showing your protégés that you care, that you are interested in their well-being, and that you are there for them.

Here are some concrete ways to be a dependable source of support:

- Provide an appropriate venue to talk in private. If none is available, go for a walk, take them to get a snack, or even play a game or sport.
- For children and younger adults, it may be helpful to do an activity while talking, such as coloring, playing ball, clay modeling.

- Use good listening skills when your protégé opens up about personal struggles—be attentive and maintain good eye contact.
- Do not multi-task when you are listening to your protégé.
- Be receptive to listening to your protégés' struggles—don't dismiss their concerns or stop them from talking about personal issues.
- Ask appropriate questions to get a true understanding of their situation. Do not assume *anything* about their reality or experiences.
- Provide reassurance when your protégés are in distress—state your confidence in their abilities to rebound.
- Tell them you care about them. You might say, "I care about you. I'm here for you." These statements of caring are simple, but mean a lot.
- If appropriate, briefly share your own struggles so they know you understand and that they are not alone. But do not monopolize the time to talk about yourself.
- If a stressful life event happens to your protégé, call them and check on them.
- If your protégés have problems that are beyond your capability to help, discuss with them if they would like to be referred to a counselor or to people who have gone through similar predicaments. This step requires you to intuit the right timing—do this too soon and your protégé might feel rejected or labeled. You might want to seek consultation if you are unsure when or how to make a referral.

Chapter 10

Telling about Yourself

You give but little when you give of your possessions.
It is when you give of yourself that you truly give.

—Kahlil Gibran (as cited in Book of Positive Quotations, 1993, p. 115)

CASE EXAMPLE: HOW ONE MENTOR'S STORIES HELPED HIS PROTÉGÉ

Short, skinny, and meek, Adisa was a target for bullying in junior high. Even the younger kids mercilessly taunted every aspect of him, from his wispy afro to his threadbare sneakers. To escape his tormenters, Adisa hid in the classroom during recess. None of the teachers could persuade him to venture into the school playground, even on the sunniest day.

Adisa's bleak life improved when his woodshop teacher invited him to use the woodshop during recess. Mr. Gonzalez, a towering tree-trunk of a man with an army sergeant's voice, could not have been more different than Adisa. Yet, the two found a common interest in woodworking. Mr. Gonzalez noticed Adisa's natural affinity with wood. He calculated angles with ease, cut his pieces precisely, and mastered all the woodworking equipment in no time at all. While other students were content making simple cutting boards, Adisa produced intricately carved wooden clocks and furniture that looked more like art pieces than a junior high project. Mr. Gonzalez helped Adisa enter his pieces in nationwide woodworking contests and cheered him onto multiple victories.

At the beginning, Adisa was guarded with Mr. Gonzalez. Over time, he grew to like and trust Mr. Gonzalez as a respected advisor and mentor. Here are several key things that Mr. Gonzalez did to foster a close mentoring relationship with Adisa:

- He opened his woodshop during recess for Adisa, giving him a safe place to hang out (see Chapter 3, Being Available).
- He showed interest in Adisa, asking him questions about his life. He got to know Adisa's family and the stories of their lives (See Chapter 6, Holistic Understanding).
- He taught him the craft of woodworking, paying close attention to his work, and giving him feedback to hone his skill (See Chapter 18, Giving Quality Feedback).
- He gave him positive feedback, boosting Adisa's confidence that he could be good at this craft (See Chapter 17, Building Confidence).
- He took Adisa's woodworking skills to a whole new level by helping him enter woodworking contests (See Chapter 22, Providing Opportunities).

Another subtle but important thing that Mr. Gonzalez did was share stories of his own life. While they were sanding wood or sweeping up saw-dust, Mr. Gonzalez told Adisa how he too used to be teased in school because of his accent and how he survived the teasing. He described how everyone had written him off because of his learning disability, and how he took steps to overcome his challenges. He also described his initial gaffes as a wood-worker, like how he simply could not pronounce a funny-sounding name of one woodworking tool.

Mr. Gonzalez's stories often included a teaching point about woodworking, school, or life. Just as importantly, these stories enabled Adisa to get to know Mr. Gonzalez as a person and not just as a teacher. Adisa began to trust him as a result.

Said Mr. Gonzalez: "It's not a secret that I'm a first generation Latino. That is always on the table with my students and with me. I think it's important for them to feel that I'm aware of who they are, and how important that is to me, and how necessary it is for them also to value that. So I don't shy away from talking about ethnic minority issues."

It would not be an exaggeration to say that Mr. Gonzalez changed the course of Adisa's life. The many recesses they spent in the woodshop eventually resulted in Adisa getting an apprenticeship in a cabinet-making company.

Adisa went on to become a much sought-after cabinet-maker, renowned for his ability to create almost anything from wood. To this day, Adisa and his former teacher still meet regularly in the old woodshop at school, trading woodworking tips, wisecracks, and, of course, personal stories.

WHY TELLING ABOUT YOURSELF MATTERS

Telling your protégé about yourself is a powerful way of teaching and passing on knowledge. Even stories of failure, personal limitations, and making mistakes provide valuable lessons on how to handle difficulties and setbacks.

Most importantly, telling stories allows your protégé to learn about you, thus setting the stage for closeness and trust. In cross-cultural relationships, it is vitally important that you enter into your protégés' worlds *and* give them the opportunity to understand your world. Only then can you achieve a mutual understanding and respect for each other.

However, there's a line between appropriate and inappropriate self-disclosure. That line is crossed when you, the mentor, divulge personal information that benefits *you* rather than your protégé. Do *not* put your protégé in the uneasy position of being your therapist, counselor, priest, minister, or rabbi—your protégé should not have to listen to your problems and feel responsible for your welfare.

PRACTICAL STRATEGIES FOR TELLING ABOUT YOURSELF

Here are some strategies for appropriate self-disclosure:

- Share stories about yourself—especially stories of your successes and failures in your professional and personal life and stories of how you dealt with challenges.
- When you share a story, explain why you are sharing the story. This will help both you and your protégé be clear about the purpose of your story.
- Don't be afraid to tell stories of your mistakes or missteps if these are insightful to your protégé.
- Disclose parts of your identity that relate to your protégé, such as juggling motherhood with school or work, being a minority in a group, or being different.
- Don't talk *too* much about yourself—remember that the reason for telling stories about yourself is to enhance your protégé's learning. Back off if your protégé seems bored.
- Be deliberate about what you choose to disclose—this point bears repeating—the purpose of self-disclosure is to benefit the protégé, not yourself. Do *not* make your protégés feel like your psychotherapist or

best friend by disclosing or burdening them with details they do not need to know.

- Before sharing a personal story, be clear about your intention for sharing the story. Ask yourself these questions:

  1. Does my story support my protégé's personal and educational professional development?
  2. How does my story support my protégé's personal and educational professional development?

Chapter 11

Acknowledging Limitations

If you do not tell the truth about yourself you cannot tell it about other people.

—Virginia Woolf (as cited in *Book of Positive Quotations,* 1993, p. 215)

CASE EXAMPLE: HOW ONE MENTOR'S ACKNOWLEDGMENT OF LIMITATIONS WAS THE "GREATEST THING"

Rita describes herself as "a way cool Deaf Aeronautics Engineer Woman." She is proud of being part of the Deaf culture and wouldn't change her condition one iota.

Growing up in a Hearing family, Rita is comfortable both in the Hearing world and in the Deaf community. It was no big deal for her to pursue an engineering degree in a college that did not have a significant Deaf population.

As a Deaf woman in a male-dominated, Hearing-dominated field, she was a double minority in her field. However, her eagerness to learn and passion for engineering quickly earned the respect and liking of both her peers and teachers.

One of her professors took an interest in her and was her chief source of support and mentoring during her undergraduate years. His knowledge about Deaf culture was instrumental in cementing their mentoring relationship.

He was also proactive in his mentoring of her, giving her tremendous career opportunities such as inviting her to be part of his research team, taking

49

her to engineering conferences, helping her get summer jobs, and spending lots of time with her to help her refine her ideas. His mentoring helped her shape and define her dream to be an aeronautics engineer.

However, as a Hearing person and as a man, he knew that he could not possibly understand and meet all her needs as a Deaf woman. To fill the gaps, he introduced her to Deaf and female colleagues, both in industry as well as in college. These colleagues formed an additional network of support for Rita.

Said Robert, Rita's mentor: "I encouraged her to connect with the Society of Women Engineers and with Deaf engineers across the country and abroad. There are just things about being a Deaf woman that I just won't know, that I have not personally experienced. So I told her it would be a good idea for her to connect with different people so she'd have professional role models. She thought that was huge that I was willing to say, 'I can't teach you everything.'

Rita echoed Robert's words, saying it was the "greatest thing" anyone had ever said to her: "We discussed our differences and how that was going to contribute to the relationship. He was very honest with me and he said one of the most honest things I've ever heard someone say. He told me point-blank: 'I'm 100 percent there for you. But I think that you should get yourself a second mentor who is Deaf and is a woman, who understands what it's like to be a Deaf woman engineer and who can guide you through that process and be a role model and give you support as well.' I really appreciate that he took the time to mentor me *and* help me get my needs met through other people."

WHY ACKNOWLEDGING LIMITATIONS MATTERS

In a mentoring relationship it is easy for protégés to set their mentors on a pedestal.

However, no mentor can meet a protégé's every need. Each mentor has areas of strengths and expertise as well as areas where they are less knowledgeable.

Instead of pretending or aspiring to be an expert in everything, it is important that mentors recognize their limitations and take steps to compensate for any lack in their mentoring.

By being open about the limits of your experience, you can pave the way for honesty and dialogue in your mentoring relationships. A conversation about your limitations can also help dispel unrealistic expectations that you are perfect and flawless in every way.

PRACTICAL SUGGESTIONS FOR
DEALING WITH YOUR LIMITATIONS

Outstanding mentoring does not mean you know everything!

Be aware of the areas in which you are limited in knowledge and expertise. Think comprehensively of the different facets of your protégé's life that may impact his or her life, school, and work goals (see Table 6.1). Take stock of all the areas in which you may not be of optimal help to your protégé, including:

- gender
- race
- ethnicity
- sexual orientation
- family obligations and responsibilities
- community obligations and responsibilities
- religion
- spirituality
- financial issues
- specific academic and work skills, such as computer, cooking, sewing, writing, job interviewing.
- social skills, such as networking, meeting people
- immigration status
- abilities and disabilities
- health conditions
- specific personal or family circumstances, such as being in a military family, being undocumented, being the first to go to high school or college
- parenting, childrearing, care-giving for elders and other care issues

Disclose your areas of strength as well as your limitations.

Educate yourself about key areas of your protégé's life where you have limited experience. Seek consultation.

Introduce your protégé to people who can help in your areas of limitation.

Encourage your protégé to participate in conferences and organizations where they can meet additional role models.

Chapter 12

Acknowledging and Repairing Mistakes

Intelligence is not to make no mistakes, but quickly to see how to make them good.

—Bertolt Brecht (as cited in *Book of Positive Quotations*, 1993, p. 662)

CASE EXAMPLE: HOW ONE MENTOR'S MISTAKES EARNED HIS PROTÉGÉ'S RESPECT

Jamal's face lights up whenever he talks about his mentor. It is clear that he has the highest respect and affection for Dr. Franklin, a pioneering African American mathematician, scholar, and professor. As one of a handful of African American mathematicians in the entire country when he started out, Dr. Franklin is committed to mentoring up-and-coming scholars. Dr. Franklin has taken many students under his wing—his only requirements are that they have a love for mathematics and are willing to work hard.

Jamal notes that Dr. Franklin is at heart a down-to-earth, humble man, despite being a luminary in the field of mathematics.

"The moment we met," said Jamal, "he told me not to put him on a pedestal. I even remember him saying, "I'm not perfect. Just don't come around me with that because then you're setting me up for failure!! But I do have some strengths. Now if we could relate around those, we can flow."

"I respected him for that—for not being all high and mighty about himself."

"He is willing to acknowledge when he makes mistakes—like when he was late for our meeting yesterday. He apologized right away, instead of denying it or blaming me."

Dr. Franklin has told Jamal stories about mistakes he has made, both in his own career and in mentoring others. For instance, he admits one occasion when he set the bar too high. He had asked one protégé to organize an applied mathematics conference, thinking this experience would be an excellent addition to the individual's resume. The protégé did the job poorly, and their relationship was strained as a result. In hindsight, Dr. Franklin admitted that the protégé was inadequately prepared for the task. Dr. Franklin took personal responsibility for the failed project and for the fallout.

Dr. Franklin's stories of failure have not diminished Jamal's respect for him. Instead, they have been powerful illustrations of how a person with tremendous status and power can still make mistakes, yet handle slip-ups with integrity, grace, and dignity.

Jamal adds that he has learned from Dr. Franklin's humility and is quick to acknowledge his own mistakes. He doesn't hide his errors or keep secrets from his mentor. As a result of their willingness to be open with each other, they have between them a deep reserve of understanding and mutual respect that can override the occasional misstep.

WHY ACKNOWLEDGING MISTAKES MATTERS

A healthy relationship does *not* mean a complete absence of conflict, argument, and setbacks. Rather, a basis for relationship health is how people handle differences, errors, and hurts when they occur. Misunderstandings and mistakes are more likely to happen in cross-cultural relationships. This is normal and expected. You *can* have a healthy cross-cultural relationship, even with the occasional slip-up.

A healthy relationship is one where both parties leave room and understanding for human error and limitations. Another marker of a healthy relationship is each individual's ability to handle setbacks and repair hurts in a mature, respectful fashion.

Some mentors and protégés might have the expectation that a good mentoring relationship is mistake- and conflict-free. Some mentors may put too much pressure on themselves to be the perfect role model and never make a mistake.

Likewise, some protégés might set their mentors up for perfection. Such expectations are unrealistic and problematic. Of course the mentor should strive to role-model good professional and personal conduct. However, the mentor is also human and is liable to make mistakes.

Remember that useful role-modeling also includes lessons in how to handle mistakes and how to take ownership for mistakes. How the mentor responds to his or her own mistakes teaches protégés what to do when they screw up. These lessons are invaluable pointers on how to be graceful under distress and how to take responsibility for one's actions.

Even the youngest protégés deserve an apology if they've been wronged. You don't have to make an elaborate apology to a child, but a sincere "I'm sorry" lets the child know you take responsibility for the mistake.

PRACTICAL STRATEGIES FOR HANDLING MISTAKES

Some Do's and Don'ts:

Do's:

- Remind yourself mistakes are inevitable; even great mentors slip-up now and then.
- Talk about the mistakes you've made to help your protégé learn how you handle mistakes.
- Realize when you have made a mistake.
- Apologize when you make a mistake or let your protégé down.
- Fix the mistake you made; make it up to your protégé in some way.
- Deal with the mistake and move on.
- Invite your protégés to be upfront with you when you've made a mistake.

Don'ts:

- Don't get defensive.
- Don't blame your protégés or insinuate it is their fault when you've made a mistake.
- Don't deny that you made the mistake.
- Don't skirt the issue or pretend nothing happened.
- Don't obsess about your mistakes—fix them and move on.

Chapter 13

Using Humor

Among those whom I like or admire, I can find no common denominator,
but among those whom I love, I can: all of them make me laugh.

—W. H. Auden (as cited in *Chambers Dictionary of*
Quotations, 1997, p. 48)

CASE EXAMPLE: HOW ONE MENTOR'S HUMOR
PUT HER PROTÉGÉ AT EASE

Macro Comp is a software company that actively recruits minorities and
women through its internship/mentoring program. In the summer, high school
juniors and seniors are paired with employees. The young protégés get to
know the company, learn about the software industry, and gain some skills
along the way. The company reaps benefits in the form of happy protégés
who return to work after high school and college. These former interns are
already trained in the ways of the company and transition easily into the
workforce.

Sheryl and Lin were paired up through this program. Sheryl was a striking high school student who was tall, blond, and an avid softball player. She
easily towered over her mentor, Lin, a slightly pudgy, middle-aged Vietnamese American woman whose idea of exercise was walking to her car.

There were even more differences beneath their striking physical dispari-
ties. Lin was straight, Sheryl lesbian. Lin came from a tight-knit family who
had banded together to create a successful family business. In contrast, Sheryl
was from a single-parent home and had to help raise her two younger siblings.

Lin arrived in America on a boat from Vietnam, whereas Sheryl's part-Native heritage meant that her family had been in the United States for countless generations.

You would think that two women so outwardly and inwardly different would have little to say to each other. Yet, whenever the pair were together, their infectious laughter spoke volumes about the close connection between them.

Sheryl remembers feeling instantly at ease the first time she met Lin and they shared a joke. She was initially intimidated by the corporate environment, but the warmth of Lin's laughter dissolved her fear. The minute Lin cracked her first joke, Sheryl relaxed and knew that she'd be able to get along with Lin.

Over lunch, they had serious as well as light-hearted talks about their cultures and family backgrounds. Sheryl shared her experiences as a biracial, European/Native American person from a single-parent family. Lin regaled Sheryl with tales of her life as a second-generation, Vietnamese single woman from a huge family.

Being able to laugh together was an important key in helping them bridge their differences and establish trust and connection.

Said Sheryl: "I think humor is a very key aspect to a mentoring relationship. To be able to laugh at yourself and to be able to just laugh at silly things makes the relationship less stuffy. It enhances the trust because there's a sense of transparency that you have to have when you let go and when you joke about something. There's a risk in being open to someone. But if you're both laughing and both think it's okay, then the relationship is successful."

WHY USING HUMOR MATTERS

Sharing a laugh may not seem like much, but it actually means a lot in close relationships. When you can share a good laugh with someone, it means that you understand each other. It also means both of you feel safe to be vulnerable and laugh about life. It means a chummy agreement that you both share in the laughter. It means that each of you has agreed to be who you are. It means no pretenses and no pretensions.

In relationships where the mentor is more experienced or is radically different, the power and cultural differences can be intimidating to the protégé. However, humor and laughter can do much to reduce and bridge distance, establish trust, and promote connection.

Humor is an important tool for engaging your protégés: a story that makes them laugh is more likely to hold their attention than one that is all serious.

Some people may fear that being too light-hearted would diminish their protégés' respect. The reverse is true—if you are able to be genuine and open about yourself, you will then gain your protégé's trust and respect. Conversely, not being fully who you are sets an artificial tone to the relationship and makes it more difficult for your protégé to trust, respect, and respond to you.

Kids and young adults love humor too! In fact, one Dutch study (de Bruyn, 2004) found humor to be the best predictor of the secondary school students' acceptance of mentors.

Of course, some mentors and protégés have more serious and sedate personalities. Strike a balance between your comfort zone and your protégé's needs. Talk to your protégé about the kinds of communication each of you feels comfortable with.

PRACTICAL CONSIDERATIONS FOR USING HUMOR WITH PROTÉGÉS OF ALL AGES

Being a mentor doesn't mean that you should be serious and business-like all the time. Truly outstanding mentors aren't afraid to be themselves, to recognize the funny side of life, to acknowledge slip-ups, or to not take themselves too seriously.

Being humorous with your protégés definitely does *not* mean reciting "knock knock" jokes or spouting canned material. It simply means being genuine about who you are and not taking life too seriously.

A good yardstick for the use of humor is this question: "Would using humor in this instance add to the positive quality of the mentoring relationship?"

A humorous story about a mistake or slip-up you made can also be a tremendous teaching point for your protégés.

If you happen to be of a more serious personality, you could still be supportive of your protégés by laughing with them when they tell you funny stories. You might also want to experiment with telling a funny story of your own.

Be attentive to your protégés, and follow their lead—if they are more serious, be sensitive to their cues.

When e-mailing or texting protégés, you can use emoticons to denote humor when appropriate.

Like anything else, humor has its limits—some subjects (like sexually explicit, racist, or sexist jokes) might seriously detract and even destroy the relationship. By the same token, it's not good practice to crack mean jokes and make fun of other people.

Remember that humor is culturally-based. What may be hilarious to you may be off-putting to your protégé. If a misunderstanding occurs, respond appropriately and apologize if necessary (see Chapter 12, Acknowledging and Repairing Mistakes).

Chapter 14

Giving Gifts

When I saw the Boss later that day, I thanked him for the gift. I left tacit the other 95 percent of my gratitude. "I'm proud of you," he said, smiling. From that day, I was unafraid to ask questions—of him or my fellow staffers—and to admit when I thought I could use a hand. I was in a safe space now.

—Eric Liu (2004, p. 89)

CASE EXAMPLE:
HOW ONE MENTOR'S GIFT-GIVING TOUCHED
THE HEART OF HIS PROTÉGÉ

Jorge was the proverbial starving graduate student who worked two jobs to finance his education and help support his family. He was the first in his family to go to college and graduate school. His parents live in Puerto Rico where they work fourteen-hour days at a small convenience store.

Although Jorge admitted it was tough to balance the demands of work and school, he had a definite spark in his eyes when he talked about his dream to teach English as a second language.

His eyes also lit up when he talked about his mentor, the principal at the elementary school where Jorge is currently a teaching assistant. By all accounts, Hideo is an exceptional principal. He knows the names of each and every student and staff, cares deeply about their well-being, and is always eager to explore innovative teaching strategies.

Hideo is also extraordinary in his commitment to mentoring new teachers. He has a weekly check-in with each newcomer during their first year at the school, and takes the time to know each individual's story, hopes, and dreams. He actively supports each teacher's goals, not only through words of encouragement, but with material support as well.

Jorge smiled non-stop as he talked about being mentored by Hideo. He eagerly pointed out Hideo's generosity at every turn of the room. "Here's a comfortable chair he gave me because I have back pain," Jorge pointed to an executive chair. He then showed me a long row of ESL teaching books that Hideo had given him. He also talked enthusiastically about his research project that he was able to get off the ground with the help of seed money from Hideo.

Jorge also said that Hideo, knowing how Jorge scrimped for every dime, would sometimes treat him to coffee or a meal. Thanks to Hideo, Jorge was introduced to sushi and fell in love with it.

Jorge understands and appreciates the meaning of gift-giving in Hideo's culture. Said Jorge: "These gifts symbolize the special mentoring relationship we share. They are a way for Hideo to express his caring and support of his protégés without using any words."

WHY GIFT-GIVING MATTERS

A picture is worth a thousand words. Likewise, giving a gift says a thousand kind words to your protégé. A small gift sends a host of messages, including, "I care about you, I'm thinking about you, I support you, I'm proud of you."

In some cultures, gift giving is a highly meaningful and richly symbolic gesture. For instance, Chinese protégés might give you a little gift of food, a card, or a book—their gifts signal that you are an important person in their eyes.

If you are mentoring a protégé from a culture that values gift-giving, remember that giving and receiving gifts is a meaningful, culturally appropriate activity to them. Learn to be comfortable accepting and giving gifts as a way of expressing caring and regard.

Gift giving does not have to be a prominent feature of your mentoring relationship. Nor do your gifts have to be lavish or extravagant. Think of gift giving as an occasional highlight to support your protégés along the way and to celebrate them when they reach their goals.

PRACTICAL IDEAS FOR GIFTS

Here is a list of possible gifts that are thoughtful and supportive:

- books and magazines on subjects of their interest
- materials, textbooks, software, or other resources to help them when they are learning a challenging subject or a new skill set
- coffee, tea, ice cream, a snack, or a meal
- supplies and tools needed for their work, such as stationery, software, or art supplies
- support in the form of seed money or resources for special projects
- conference fees
- entrance or membership fees to educational sites, such as museums, art galleries
- tickets to performances (such as plays, art installations, movies, talks).

Part II

Developing the Protégé's Skills

This section focuses on the things mentors can do to support their protégés' school and/or career development. The action steps described in the following chapters will enable your protégés to enhance their professional development, build their confidence in their abilities, and help them advance academically and professionally.

As with all the practices described in this book, remember that you need to be proactive in working with your protégés. Don't wait for your protégés to ask you. Take the initiative to do the following:

- discuss dreams and goals
- build skills
- build confidence wih positive words
- give quality feedback
- give practical support
- overcome self-limiting beliefs

Chapter 15

Discussing Dreams and Goals

Hold fast to dreams, for if dreams die, life is a broken-winged bird that cannot fly.

— Langston Hughes (cited in *Book of Positive Quotations,* 1993, p. 382)

When you go to university and you are the first, you bring everyone to school with you. Your relatives and neighbors. You carry their hopes in your knapsack. Their expectations are your chaperone. Everyone is asking after you, wanting to know how you are doing, what you are learning. What you will become. You want to do something to repay them. You want to become something worthy of all that unrequited wondering.

—Eric Liu (2004, p. 128)

CASE EXAMPLE: HOW TALKING ABOUT DREAMS CHANGED THE LIFE OF ONE PROTÉGÉ

When you talk to Ron now, you would never guess the hardship that he endured growing up. An infectious laugh punctuates his speech, and his broad smile continually lights up his face. His uncanny resemblance to the golfer "Tiger Woods" quickly earned him the nickname "Tiger."

Another similarity he shares with Tiger is his mixed race family—Ron's father is European and African American, and his mother is Thai, like Tiger Woods' mom.

Ron's parents worked hard to provide a good life for their children. They wanted Ron and his sister to have good jobs and pushed them to be doctors, lawyers, or engineers.

However, their dreams were not Ron's dreams. His secret desire was to be a nurse educator. He didn't want to be a doctor, lawyer, or engineer—his passion was to work hands-on with kids and teach them about health.

Ron's career dream was not the only secret he kept from his parents. He harbored another secret that was even less aligned with his parents' dreams and hopes for him.

On his fourteenth birthday, Ron came out to them with his secret, informing them that he was gay, and begging for their support. Both parents visibly turned pale—his father with anger and his mother with shock. As fundamentalist Christians, they believed that Ron was a sinner and that homosexuality was a lifestyle choice.

From the moment Ron broke his news, his life unraveled. His mom wept daily, blaming herself for Ron's "sin." His dad maintained a stony silence that cut Ron to the core.

Things came to a head when his parents insisted that he be "deprogrammed" from homosexuality. When he refused to be "treated," they disowned him.

Out of options, Ron ran away and sought refuge in a shelter for runaway teens. At the shelter, he was embraced and accepted for who he was by his peers as well as by the shelter counselors.

One of the counselors became his mentor, friend, and adviser. Rashad, a former runaway and a Big Brother from the local Big Brothers Big Sisters program, understood what Ron was going through and took him under his wing.

The two had a blast going to baseball games, shooting hoops, playing chess, or simply going to the Dairy Queen near the shelter.

Their outings were not just about having fun and games, however. Spending time together enabled them to get to know each other and for Ron to grow to like and trust Rashad. While they shot hoops or ate their hamburgers, they had many serious discussions about Ron's life, goals, identity, and hopes.

When Rashad first asked Ron about his dreams and goals, Ron was taken aback. It was the first time anybody had shown interest in his dreams. No one—not his parents, teachers, or friends—had ever asked him that question. His parents had always assumed that they knew better than he, and that he should become a lawyer, doctor, or engineer.

Ron labored to answer, fearful Rashad might make fun of him, dash his hopes, or, worst of all, be indifferent. But the way in which Rashad responded proved that he was truly interested. When Ron hesitantly disclosed his hope of becoming a nurse educator, Rashad listened attentively and asked thoughtful questions. He gave Ron suggestions and ideas to achieve his goal.

Said Ron: "Rashad oriented me to nursing. He talked about the possibilities in nursing, about continued training, and my own interests. He gave me options that I had never really thought that much about. And he supported my efforts to pursue those options."

Their initial conversation about Ron's dreams was not a one-time event. Over the years, they had many conversations about his ongoing goals, aspirations, and hopes, including Ron's vision to start a nonprofit and his desire to form an Indie band. With each new dream that popped up, Rashad listened patiently, provided helpful input and advice, brainstormed ideas, and even offered opportunities to turn Ron's dreams into reality.

When I asked Rashad about supporting Ron's dreams, he said: "I want him to think big and do something that he'll be proud of, something that will make a contribution. I try to look at each person's potential and think about what they might shoot for. I try to have them shoot big, shoot for their dream jobs as well as some other jobs that may not be the dream job but might be a stepping-stone to a dream job. Many kids don't know the options available to them. So I make it my job to talk with them about what the possibilities are. The look in their eyes when I open up these possibilities to them . . . that look is priceless."

Ron is now at a community college pre-nursing program. His enthusiasm bubbles over as he talks about his anatomy course and the positive steps he has taken since running away. With his Big Brother's guidance, he continues to hold fast to his dream. And he continues to dream big.

WHY IT MATTERS FOR MENTORS TO TALK ABOUT DREAMS AND GOALS WITH PROTÉGÉS

Few kids (or adults) are asked, "What are your dreams for your life?"

Instead, many are asked, "What do you want to be when you grow up?"

The first question is far more powerful because it pays tribute to the deepest and highest yearnings, dreams, and aspirations of the individual.

Sadly, many of us are never even asked about our dreams. Thus, we don't get to talk about what we envision for ourselves. As a result, we tend to keep our hopes and aspirations private. Without support from others, we might doubt our abilities to fulfill our dreams.

This is why it's all the more critical that you pose this question to your protégé—"What are your dreams for your life?"

The very asking of this question says, "Your dream is important—you are important—your dream is important to me."

Outstanding mentors take the time to ask their protégés about their dreams, goals, and aspirations. This type of conversation is not a one-time event: the mentor has to invest time, energy, and interest in getting to know the protégé and his/her hopes.

It is vital that you show support, caring, and interest in your protégés' current dreams, even if they change over time. Showing genuine interest and demonstrating support is one of the keys to building trust and expressing caring.

One's dreams might not be restricted to one's life, but might also include dreams for one's family or community (such as wanting to give back to the community, or desiring to help out the family.) This is particularly true in group-oriented cultures which place a high value on looking out for each other. Be sure to ask your protégés the dreams they have for themselves as well as for the significant people in their lives.

At the same time, watch for signs that your protégés are speaking about someone else's dreams, rather than their own dreams. For example, some parents might put undue pressure on their kids to pursue specific career paths that their children are not interested in. As the mentor, help your protégés navigate the fine line between realizing their own dreams and respecting their parents' wishes.

A conversation about dreams and career possibilities can open up vistas and possibilities that your protégé may not have thought of. This may be especially true of new immigrants to this country, to students whose parents have not gone to school, or to others who have had limited exposure to different worlds. Children who grow up helping their parents in agriculture may not know there are other worlds beyond the field. Those whose parents have never gone to high school, college, or graduate school might not think of education as within their grasp. This is why it's vitally important for you to inquire about dreams, introduce new ideas, and open up new avenues to your protégés.

PRACTICAL STRATEGIES FOR TALKING ABOUT DREAMS AND GOALS

Here are some common essentials when talking about dreams and goals with protégés of any age:

- Have them fill out the "Dreams and Goals" worksheet (Table 15.1). Talk with them about their current and future dreams, as well as the obstacles that may derail their plans (Table 15.2).
- Pay attention when your protégés talk about goals and dreams. Listen with full attention, look them in the eye, stay focused on them. Remember that they might feel vulnerable when discussing their personal dreams.

- Show interest by asking thoughtful questions.
- Check in periodically about their dreams and goals—remember this is not a one-time conversation. You can do this in-person, or even via phone or e-mail.
- Be patient when dreams and goals change. Remember that this is a normal part of human development.
- Share stories of how you went about pursuing and achieving your dreams.
- Tell them how your goals changed over time.

HOW TO TALK TO YOUR PROTÉGÉS ABOUT THEIR DREAMS

Ask the following questions:

- What dreams do you have for yourself? For your family? For your community?
- What dreams does your family have for you? How are their dreams different from your dreams?
- Who are your heroes or heroines? What do you admire about them?
- What do you want to do with your life?
- What are some cool things people do for work or fun?
- What motivates you to go to school/college/graduate school/work?
- What are some things you'd like to accomplish in school/college/ graduate school?
- What do you want to do with your life after school/college?
- What might prevent you from reaching your goals?
- Imagine the perfect work day—what would that day look like? What would you be doing during this day?
- Where do you see yourself in ten years?
- Open up new possibilities. Ask: "Have you thought of . . .?" (name possibilities they might not have thought of).
- Show them what you do in your work. Invite them to your workplace. Show them the products of your work.
- Tell them what you see as their strengths and potential. "You could be really great as a . . ."
- Show support for your protégé's dreams and goals. Offer to help further these goals; for example, "That's great you love dinosaurs. How about we go to the natural science museum and see some dinosaurs?"

Table 15.1.   Dreams and Goals Worksheet

To aid discussions of dreams and goals, ask your protégé to fill out this worksheet. Ideally, both you and your protégé will have a copy of this worksheet to refer to over the course of your mentoring relationship.

My big and small dreams and goals for this year	What are obstacles to my dreams?
My big and small dreams and goals for my life	What are obstacles to my dreams?

Table 15.2.   Obstacles (Real, Imagined, or Potential) to the Protégé's Success

Suggestion: Ask your protégés to check off any issues that they are dealing with. This will enable you to have a better understanding of the challenges facing your protégés and how to help them. Another way to use this checklist is to bring up these topics with your protégés and have a conversation about how much they impact them. If the problem is severe enough to require ongoing/professional help, refer your protégés to appropriate experts (e.g. psychotherapist, physician).

For Younger Protégés

__ **Lack of motivation**
__ **Fear**
__ **Family responsibilities**
__ **Peer pressures or other problems with peers**
__ **Family dysfunction (e.g. alcoholism, drugs)**
__ **Substance abuse, addictions**
__ **Mental health issues (e.g. obsessive-compulsive disorder, anxiety)**
__ **Pressures or influences from boyfriend or girlfriend**
__ **Lack of money**
__ **Lack of knowledge about the system**
__ **Lack of confidence, low self-esteem**
__ **Lack of support from family**
__ **Lack of self-discipline**
__ **Poor study skills**
__ **Lack of resources (e.g. quiet place to study, computer, internet access, books)**
__ **Demands of family obligations**
__ **Parental pressures (e.g. to help in the family business)**
__ **Demands from work**
__ **Lack of competency in important skill areas (e.g. English, math, physical sciences)**
__ **Overconfidence**
__ **Lack of experience**
__ **Racism or discrimination**
__ **Gangs**
__ **Unsupportive teachers at school**
__ **Health or medical issues**
__ **Community obligations (e.g. church activities)**
__ **Shyness, poor social skills**
__ **False beliefs/expectations (e.g. girls are not good at math)**
__ **Pride, unwillingness to depend on others**
__ **Grief/loss**
__ **Tendency to overreact**
__ **Getting into trouble at school**
__ **High sensitivity**
__ **Disability**
__ **Other** _____

For Young Adult and Adult Protégés

__ **Lack of motivation**
__ **Fear**
__ **Family responsibilities**
__ **Influence from peers**
__ **Wanting to start a family**
__ **Pressures or influences from spouse/partner/significant other**
__ **Financial pressures, debt**
__ **Lack of knowledge about the system**
__ **Lack of confidence, low self-esteem**
__ **Lack of support from family**
__ **Family dysfunction (e.g. alcoholism, drugs)**
__ **Lack of self-discipline**
__ **Lack of resources (e.g. quiet place to work, computer, internet access, books)**
__ **Health or medical issues**
__ **Substance abuse, addictions**
__ **Mental health issues (e.g. depression, anxiety)**
__ **Demands of childrearing**
__ **Lack of childcare**
__ **Parental pressures (e.g. to help in the family business)**
__ **Job demands**
__ **Poor study skills**
__ **Lack of competency in important skill areas (e.g. writing, statistics, research)**
__ **Overconfidence**
__ **Lack of experience**
__ **Racism or discrimination**
__ **A past they are ashamed of (e.g. being fired from a job, incarceration)**
__ **Lack of network or contacts**
__ **Shyness, poor social skills**
__ **Poor self-assertiveness**
__ **False beliefs/expectations (e.g. believing they are not qualified for the job)**
__ **Pride, unwillingness to depend on others**
__ **Grief/loss**
__ **Tendency to overreact**
__ **Disability**
__ **Other** _____

Chapter 16

Building Skills

He who would learn to fly one day must first learn to stand and walk and run and climb and dance; one cannot fly into flying.

—Friedrich Nietzsche (cited in *Book of Positive Quotations*, 1993, p. 632)

CASE EXAMPLE: HOW ONE MENTOR HELPED HER PROTÉGÉ BUILD NEW SKILLS . . . AND CHANGED HER LIFE IN THE PROCESS

Lupe's initial goal was to be a high school teacher. But her first foray into teaching was a disaster. Without a mentor, she was completely unprepared for the challenges of teaching. Her students made fun of her accent. Lupe could not even get her students to stay in their seats.

Lupe felt alone in her misery and quickly became depressed and discouraged. She dreaded going to school, so much so that she threw up each morning before leaving home. Her teaching experience was so disheartening that she decided to change careers and become a psychologist.

When she entered graduate school, she was convinced that she wanted to be a clinician, believing she was not cut out for teaching. But her advisor/mentor, Constance, saw potential in her and invited her to teach a class with her.

Noticing the terror in Lupe's eyes, Constance took Lupe by the hand (both literally and figuratively). She patiently explained the syllabus and lesson plans. She showed Lupe how to deliver a lecture. She taught her how to lead discussions. She let Lupe observe first, then had Lupe co-teach with her.

75

When Lupe felt comfortable in front of the class, Constance slowly prepared Lupe to lead the class by herself. She debriefed with Lupe after each class. In those sessions, they discussed how to troubleshoot problems, such as how to handle student absences and increase class participation.

As Constance supported Lupe's teaching efforts, her confidence grew. She surprised herself by falling in love with teaching, so much so that she is now a faculty member at a teaching college.

WHY SKILL-BUILDING MATTERS

Specific skills are required at each stage of a person's professional life. Some of these skills are obvious, some are not. For instance, students taking a college-level calculus class need to have the math skills to understand and pass the class. On top of this, students need hidden skills such as time management, note-taking, punctuality, study skills, and test-taking. Lacking just one of these skills could stop the students from passing calculus and other classes.

Yet, protégés themselves might be unaware of the importance of these skills. Those from minority groups and those new to college or a profession might need extra help and support in identifying and developing these skills. Some protégés also need to learn skills when walking within two worlds. For example, some ethnic minority individuals have to learn bicultural skills when they live, study, or work in predominantly Euro-American environments. Likewise, gays and lesbians must learn how to interface in a predominantly straight environment.

Outstanding mentors work with their protégés to pinpoint skills they need to acquire or improve. Mentors do much for their protégés' skill development when they provide individualized support, advice, and coaching. Building up a protégé's skill can be done in practical, simple ways. For instance, you can invite your protégés to collaborate with you on a project. Through close supervision, training, and collaboration, protégés can master skills and gain confidence.

PRACTICAL STRATEGIES FOR BUILDING
SKILLS WITH ALL PROTÉGÉS

- *Before* discussing skill-building, be sure to have at least one conversation about your protégés' dreams and goals so you'll have a road-map of where they want to go.
- Discuss the skills your protégés want to learn.

- Map out the different skills they need to acquire.
- Explain or show the benefits of having specific skills in their current setting.
- Ask about hidden skills that protégés need to develop.
- Explain the process of developing a skill; break the process into manageable steps.
- Tell stories about how you developed your own skills.
- Provide challenging assignments and other opportunities for your protégés to develop skills.
- Collaborate with protégés; involve them in your own projects if possible.
- Provide advice, support, coaching, and feedback as they develop their skills.
- Provide concrete help as needed, such as supplies, examples of work, etc.
- When necessary, introduce protégés to people who are willing and able to help them build skills.
- Check periodically with your protégés about their progress in skill-building.
- Help protégés figure out financial issues and any barriers to building certain skills.
- Provide feedback and encouragement when protégés feel discouraged or challenged.
- Never assume that your protégés know all the skills they need to learn.
- Never assume that your protégés know how to go about developing their skills.

SKILL-BUILDING STRATEGIES FOR K–12 PROTÉGÉS

- Typical skills to help build for this age group: math, English, languages, reading, writing, music, art, sports, science, social sciences, job market skills (writing a resume, looking for a job, interviewing), and college preparatory skills (taking Advanced Placement courses, applying for college, writing the college essay, applying for scholarships and financial aid).
- Don't forget hidden skills such as study skills, test-taking skills, social skills, time management, dealing with bullies, and Internet/online skills.
- Never underestimate your protégés at this stage of the game—they might be interested in learning many other skills beyond school, such as entrepreneurship skills, public speaking, or even creating a nonprofit or small business.

SKILL-BUILDING STRATEGIES FOR COLLEGE
AND GRADUATE STUDENT PROTÉGÉS

- Typical skills to help build for this group: writing, critical thinking, math/ statistics, research, publishing, teaching, presenting, reviewing, job entry skills, graduate school applications.
- Don't forget basic skills that protégés might have trouble with, such as balancing school, work, and personal life, organizational skills, people skills such as interacting with professors and peers.
- Collaboration is especially helpful with this population—share authorship, involve students in teaching, writing, research, and presenting.

SKILL-BUILDING STRATEGIES FOR TEACHERS
IN TRAINING PROTÉGÉS

- Typical skills to help build for this group: preparing lesson plans, curriculum design, leading group discussions, scaffolding, grading, counseling students, dealing with challenging students, classroom management, and working with parents and fellow teachers.
- Discuss less obvious skills that can be critical to success in the profession (such as interfacing with principals and administration, committee work, and performance at staff meetings).
- Discuss any additional skills they would like to acquire, such as research, administration.
- Observe your protégés in the classroom and give them feedback.
- Ask to see samples of their work (such as grading, lesson plans, syllabus) and discuss these with them.
- Invite your protégés to collaborate with you on professional projects.

SKILL-BUILDING STRATEGIES FOR WORKFORCE PROTÉGÉS

- Address specific job skills. For instance, nurses must learn specialized skills such as monitoring blood pressure, managing caseloads, and trach care.
- Address general work skills such as writing, computer skills, financial skills, supervising, presenting, interpersonal and teamwork skills, customer service, and phone skills.

- Discuss less obvious work skills that can be critical to success, such as time management, dealing with office politics, personal conduct, interacting with colleagues, making small talk, working efficiently, and following instructions.
- Discuss and provide support for developing new skills that will encourage promotion.
- Invite your protégés to participate in your projects to aid skill development.

Chapter 17

Building Confidence with Positive Words

I've learned that people will forget what you said, people will forget what you did, but people will never forget how you made them feel.

— Maya Angelou (1998)

CASE EXAMPLE: HOW ONE MENTOR'S POSITIVE WORDS INSPIRED HER PROTÉGÉ AND KEPT HER GOING

Mei Li, an international student from China, had a hard time adjusting to life in the United States and to her new life as a doctoral student in a top research university. She desperately missed her family in China. On top of this, she did not fit in with her peers, an elite group of twenty-somethings who came from upper-middle class families and had graduated from Ivy League institutions. Mei Li, on the other hand, was an older student, who had left her husband and young son to get her degree in America.

To make matters worse, she was in an extremely competitive program that made no attempts to be warm and fuzzy. Quite the reverse, the faculty took pride in being critical and tough. Mei Li's first student review left her in tears. She had worked herself into a frenzy to prepare for it, yet her committee made zero compliments and instead demanded additional measures to improve her work.

After her tough review, Mei Li slunk to her student apartment, wondering if she should drop out of academia. When she arrived home, she spotted a letter from her mentor in her mailbox. Written in elegant script, her mentor reminded her about her achievements, including her dedication to her son and family in China. Her note ended with the words "You're doing great. I'm proud of you."

Mei Li's spirits revived as she read those affirming words. Her mentor's positive affirmation soothed the sting of the scathing review—it was like her personal cheerleader had materialized at just the right time, encouraging and urging her on. Her mentor's caring words erased the hurt from the review and at the same time shored up Mei Li's confidence and belief in herself.

Mei Li carried that letter in her purse till the very last day of her doctoral program when she walked across the stage to receive her diploma, her head held high. One of the people cheering her achievement in the audience was, of course, her mentor.

WHY GIVING POSITIVE FEEDBACK MATTERS

The emotional support of family and friends is important, but positive feedback from mentors holds special meaning. It's the difference between your Mom saying "You did a good job," and your boss saying the exact same words. Mom's words feel good but they don't have the same weight of validation and authority of your boss' words.

A mentor's positive words carry an appreciation and understanding of the degree of pain, hard work, and sacrifice involved. These encouraging words can do much to boost your protégé's confidence and to stay the course.

Words like "I'm proud of you" or "You did a great job with that essay" can mean the world to a protégé. It feels good to know that one's existence is cherished. It feels good to know that someone notices and takes pride in one's accomplishments. It means a lot to know that someone cares.

A mentor's support is especially important when the protégé undertakes a project that is deeply meaningful to them, yet is not fully supported by others. When people choose to embark on a project—whether the project is an elementary school show-and-tell, a college paper, or a work presentation—they often pick topics that are close to the heart. If a lesbian student wanted to do a high school project about gay and lesbian issues, it's a pretty safe bet she has chosen this topic because it is deeply meaningful to her. If an African American graduate student decides to study resiliency in minority populations, it is very probable that the topic has profound personal significance that goes beyond a professional interest.

Yet, such projects are sometimes denigrated or devalued in direct and indirect ways. One protégé told me her colleagues had dismissed her research on Asian Americans as "bullshit." Another student was steered away from doing a fieldwork project focusing on Latino/Latina issues.

It can mean the world to your protégés when you take the time to express enthusiasm and support for their work, particularly if their work is not universally respected. Such support is a powerful affirmation and validation of their professional and personal interests.

Building confidence does not mean manufacturing or faking praise. Do not say positive words just for the sake of being nice. Instead, take the opportunity to give positive feedback only when it is warranted and when you can speak from the heart.

PRACTICAL STRATEGIES FOR BUILDING YOUR PROTÉGÉS' CONFIDENCE WITH POSITIVE WORDS

- The message is simple—say, write, or e-mail positive words when appropriate.
- Notice when your protégé is doing well or making good effort and take the time to give positive feedback.
- Never underestimate the power of words such as, "I'm proud of you," "You did a great job."
- There is no such thing as too much praise when your protégé achieves a hard won goal.
- Be specific in your praise, such as, "I like how you . . . ," "You did such a good job in . . . ." Feedback that is specific is more helpful and authentic to the protégé than general statements such as, "You're great."
- Note and praise effort as well as achievement. Let your protégés know that you recognize their hard work regardless of whether it pays off.

Chapter 18

Giving Quality Feedback

With Robert, everything had to be perfect. Every dish, every piece of fish seared properly, every vegetable blanched and seasoned perfect, every chicken breast roasted with herbs as exactly as he showed us. . . . I was mesmerized, inspired, and motivated by him. He not only taught me how to cook, but how to behave, how to conduct myself among the top professionals in the industry. He talked to me about my walk. "Your walk is too hard," he said. "You need to ease up a bit—people take notice."

—Jeff Henderson (2007, p. 195)

CASE EXAMPLE: A MENTOR GIVES QUALITY FEEDBACK

"It's useless to me if someone gives me generic feedback, like "That's great!" or "You write well!" exclaimed Kumar, a small-built high school student with a big presence. Kumar was busy applying for colleges. He had just finished writing his personal statement.

"I sent it out to ten people and asked them for feedback. Nine of the ten said things like "That's great!" or "You did a good job!" Those people were nice but they didn't help me at all.

"Only my mentor gave me concrete feedback that helped me improve my essay. I mean, he *really* helped me."

I took a look at the comments Kumar's mentor had penciled on his draft. I was struck by the care he'd lavished on giving him feedback.

His mentor had given detailed suggestions and questions for every paragraph. He told Kumar which parts were strong and which needed re-working. Most importantly, he explained *why*.

The quality of his mentor's feedback was outstanding. Plus, the thoughtfulness of the feedback showed that he not only recognized the importance of the essay, but was invested in helping Kumar improve it.

Excitedly drumming his hands on the table, Kumar said, "He helped me write the best possible essay I could write. In the process, he helped me become a better writer. I'm really proud of that essay now. I feel good about applying to college with that essay."

WHY GIVING QUALITY FEEDBACK MATTERS

The previous chapter discussed the importance of building your protégé's confidence through positive words. Giving quality feedback includes positive words as well as constructive criticism. Giving quality feedback is essential for enabling the protégé to develop and grow. I use the word "quality" to emphasize that the mentor should provide comments and observations that are specific, constructive, and detailed.

In contrast, generic or vague feedback is unhelpful at best. At worst, poor feedback can adversely affect the mentoring relationship. One research study found that protégés who received insufficient feedback felt their mentors were keeping them at arm's length. Thus, the gesture of giving quality, in-depth feedback not only supports the protégé's growth, it is also a powerful way of demonstrating caring and interest and maintaining trust.

PRACTICAL STRATEGIES FOR GIVING QUALITY FEEDBACK

Provide feedback in a detailed and precise manner, noting areas for improvement and suggestions for strengthening the work. Tell them the *why* (the reason behind your feedback) and the *how* (ideas for corrective action). An example of a detailed, concrete, constructive response would be:

> "This [specify what it is] needs work because [state the reasons] and maybe one way to improve this is for you to [suggest actions]."

This formula for giving feedback enables protégés to understand where their weak spots are and how they can move to the next level.

Feedback that is too global or generic is of little use. For instance, it is not that helpful when people say "You're great!" or "This needs work," and leave it at that. These statements do not give protégés specific feedback about their performance.

It's far more helpful to give clear detail about where, how, and why your protégé did well. For example, instead of saying "This is good!" a more insightful and helpful comment might be, "I liked how you structured the introduction and gave it a compelling opening line."

You might understandably be concerned about hurting your protégés' feelings or that protégés might receive your feedback negatively. You might have a legitimate fear about being perceived as being harsh or critical. Particularly, in cross-racial relationships, mentors might hesitate from giving constructive criticism because they fear that their protégés feel offended or might misinterpret their comments.

However, research in cross-racial pairs has shown that feedback will be positively received when the mentor meets four conditions:

1. Begins with the positives
2. Clearly expresses high expectations
3. Believes in the protégés' ability to achieve those standards
4. Communicates a deep desire to help protégés reach their potential.

Hence, to help ensure that your constructive criticism is received well, make sure that you express your caring for your protégés' growth, state your high expectations of them, and tell them you believe in their potential to achieve high standards.

Finally, don't wait for protégés to ask for feedback—*offer* to give them feedback. Ask them: "Would you like my feedback on this?" Being proactive about offering feedback is yet another way to demonstrate caring.

K–12 PROTÉGÉS: AREAS FOR GIVING FEEDBACK

• school assignments and projects
• after-school activities
• extracurricular activities
• hobbies
• personal conduct
• job applications

PRE-COLLEGE, COLLEGE AND GRADUATE STUDENT PROTÉGÉS: AREAS FOR GIVING FEEDBACK

• college assignments and projects
• essays

- college application essays
- scholarship essays
- personal conduct
- job applications
- portfolios

TEACHERS IN TRAINING PROTÉGÉS: AREAS FOR GIVING FEEDBACK

- syllabus construction
- curriculum development and planning
- lesson plans
- homework assignments
- grading
- disciplinary measures
- classroom management
- teaching performance
- performance on committees
- teaching portfolios

WORKFORCE PROTÉGÉS: AREAS FOR GIVING FEEDBACK

- job performance on specific work duties
- writing (both paper and e-mail)
- time management
- task management
- communication skills
- special work projects
- personal conduct
- performance in meetings
- teamwork performance
- performance on committees and boards (both internal and external)
- interpersonal relationships
- supervision and management skills

Chapter 19

Giving Practical Support

I had a little help from a teacher named Herman Katz. He turned out to be one of those adult male role models my mother was always seeking. . . . He got me to study for the SATs. He even offered to pay for me to take the SATs, and he really helped me focus on college and pushed me to apply. I ended up going to UCLA in large part because of him. He was a wonderful man—a real mentor, a real inspiration—and I talk about him everywhere I go.

—Antonio Villaraigosa, *Mayor of The City of Los Angeles*
(Washington & Paisner, 2006, p. 245)

CASE EXAMPLE: HOW ONE MENTOR PROVIDED PRACTICAL SUPPORT

Winona was a first-generation Native American college student whose family lives on a South Dakota reservation. Winona's dream was to be a professor of Native American history so she could teach and help preserve her culture and history.

Winona's mentor, a professor of African history, took Winona under her wing when she noticed Winona's enthusiasm for history. Although their interests were different, Winona's mentor showed her support by giving her articles and books on Native American history. She paid for Winona to attend history conferences that Winona would not otherwise have known about, let alone afford to go.

Knowing that Winona worked two part-time jobs on top of going to school full-time, her mentor treated her to coffee or a meal when they met at a café. She regularly forwarded information about scholarships and workshops, such as a free GRE preparation workshop that boosted Winona's graduation school application.

Winona showed me the latest gift from her mentor—a GRE workbook that her mentor highly recommended and bought for her. Said Winona, "It's so thoughtful of her to think of me. And it makes me feel good that she's thinking of me. I love that she thinks of my needs and sends me things without me having to ask for them."

WHY GIVING PRACTICAL SUPPORT MATTERS

Mentors can provide practical support in many different ways. Giving a book, lending the right tool, sharing a lesson plan, showing how a software program works, or providing work samples are a few ways in which mentors can support their protégés.

Pointing the protégé to helpful resources is another form of practical support.

When protégés are struggling to pay for education or training, the occasional help from a mentor can be a lifesaver. For students new to school, college, or the workplace, the practical support of mentors is especially critical because they and their families might be completely unaware of the various forms of help available to them. For example, a first-generation Latina going to college might not know about support resources like Financial Aid, Extended Opportunity Programs, or even academic advising.

Providing practical support means giving or lending the tools to empower protégés along their journey. The critical piece in providing practical support is *empowerment:* remember that the overarching goal of mentoring is to guide your protégé toward growth and resiliency, *not* to create dependency.

Being a good mentor *doesn't* mean that you bankroll your protégé's career. A good mentor does not immediately offer money as a quick-fix.

At critical moments when the lack of funds could lead to a serious backslide, it would be appropriate to offer direct help. However, in most cases, the first order of business is to help protégés stand on their own feet and become knowledgeable about institutional resources.

Here are some action steps to take before providing practical support:

1. Ask your protégés if there are any constraints preventing them from achieving their short-term and long-term goals.

2. Discuss and strategize with your protégés how they can manage these obstacles.
3. Point them to existing resources.
4. Offer practical help as appropriate.

PRACTICAL SUPPORT IDEAS FOR K–12 PROTÉGÉS

- Tell them about resources for books, scholarships, free classes, and fee waivers, such as www.fastweb.com.
- Discuss their financial needs during summer months and how they can manage their needs.
- Provide examples of written work, such as scholarship essays.
- Lend or give books and articles, tools, software, and other material resources.
- Refer to community agencies that are set up to provide aid and other resources, such as Boys & Girls Clubs, Girls Inc.

PRACTICAL SUPPORT IDEAS FOR PRE-COLLEGE, COLLEGE, AND GRADUATE STUDENT PROTÉGÉS

- Tell them about resources for scholarships, books, and fee waivers. In particular, tell them about scholarships targeted toward specific groups, such as a Hispanic Scholarship Fund or an American Indian College Fund.
- Explore financial aid options, such as Federal aid, grants, loans, and scholarships.
- Offer research and teaching assistantships.
- Discuss their financial needs during summer months and how they can manage their needs.
- Provide seed money or point them to resources for starting research and community projects.
- Provide examples of written work, such as conference handouts, Power Point slides, and application essays for college and graduate school.
- Tell them about local and national community agencies that are set up to provide aid, such as Youth Uprising in Oakland, California, or the American Association of University Women.
- Discuss extracurricular expenses and how to meet them, such as applying for scholarships to attend conference.

• Lend or give books and articles, tools, software, and other material resources.

PRACTICAL SUPPORT IDEAS FOR TEACHER-IN-TRAINING PROTÉGÉS

• Point them to resources for scholarships, books, fee waivers, and loan forgiveness programs, such as the Phi Delta Kappa International Education Foundation awards for education students.
• Explore financial aid options, such as Federal aid, grants, loans, and teaching scholarships.
• Provide examples of work, such as syllabuses, lesson plans, and handouts.
• Lend or give tools they can use in the classroom, such as classroom materials.
• Lend or give books and articles on teaching and professional development.
• Provide seed money or point them to resources for starting research and community projects.
• Point them to resources designated for teachers, such as: http://www.donorschoose.org/ or www.raft.net.
• Point them to specific teaching support Web sites and newsgroups for additional information.

PRACTICAL SUPPORT IDEAS FOR WORKFORCE PROTÉGÉS

• Discuss resources for enhancing work skills, such as continuing education opportunities, professional conferences, and community college courses.
• Show samples of work projects, such as presentation materials, speeches.
• Lend or provide tools to develop work skills, such as software programs, books, and tools.
• Point them to job-specific internet sites that offer professional support, such as http://allnurses.com/ for nurses, or http://www.bmes.org/careers.asp for biomedical engineers.

Chapter 20

Overcoming Self-Limiting Beliefs

Your success depends mainly upon what you think of yourself and whether you believe in yourself.

—William J. H. Boetcker (as cited in *Book of Positive Quotations*, 1993, p. 242)

CASE EXAMPLE: A MENTOR HELPS HER PROTÉGÉ OVERCOME SELF-LIMITING BELIEFS AND ACHIEVE HIS POTENTIAL

Seung is a second-generation Korean American student whose parents immigrated in hopes of a better life for their children. Much of Seung's childhood was spent in his family's little convenience store. His parents worked at the shop every single day of the week, including Christmas and New Year's Day. Most work days began at 5 a.m. and ended midnight or later.

Working hard was a way of life as well as an ingrained cultural value for Seung's family. His mother would often refer to the Korean proverb "One can build a mountain by collecting specks of dust" to illustrate that Seung could achieve anything, if he were diligent.

Seung followed his parents' example of working hard and graduated top of his class with a business degree. He landed a job in a Big Five accounting firm. True to his upbringing, he put in exhaustive hours, often completing projects in record time.

He was the most productive of his peers, yet was passed over for promotion time and again. He became depressed, believing he was incapable of achieving success at the corporate level.

Seung's career might have stagnated endlessly had not a new supervisor arrived and taken him under her wing. Despite vast differences in race, culture, gender, and upbringing, the pair developed a great mentoring relationship because of their deep respect for each other.

Seung's mentor noticed that he tended to brush off any compliments and underplay his achievements, modestly stating that he was just a "hard worker." She saw that he never volunteered to take on a new assignment nor did he tell his colleagues or supervisors about the additional work projects he quietly undertook. Time and again, less competent but more confident co-workers angled for plum assignments and subsequently got promoted over him.

Over many conversations, Seung's mentor accrued a deep understanding of his cultural values. Seung explained how his parents' example had shown him the value of hard work. He believed that his hard work spoke for itself and that it was pushy and impolite to trumpet his achievements or ask for assignments and promotions. During their conversations, Seung's mentor saw that he attributed all his success to hard work, and gave zero credit to his intelligence, competence, and skills.

Instead of denouncing his cultural values and beliefs, she offered an alternative viewpoint of his strengths that could co-exist with his cultural beliefs. She said to Seung: "The American business world may at first glance run totally counter to your cultural values. But you can find a way to be true to yourself and to your culture and still be a shining success in the business and corporate world."

Seung and his mentor talked at length about strategies for him to achieve this. One method that Seung felt comfortable with was to take the time to get to know each of his superiors and to allow them to get to know him on a one-to-one basis. By doing so, Seung was able to showcase his strengths in an authentic manner that did not feel like he was brown-nosing.

Seung's mentor also enlarged his beliefs about himself by reminding him of tangible achievements that he had accomplished. In doing so, Seung received positive feedback that he started to internalize and believe. He began to take credit for accomplishments that he would have otherwise dismissed.

By gently expanding Seung's beliefs, his mentor helped him see a richer and more accurate perspective of himself and his abilities. At the same time, she shored up his confidence and taught him to be bicultural.

With effective mentoring, Seung rose up the corporate ladder in a way that was aligned with his temperament and cultural codes. He became a much-liked manager who was deeply respected for his competence, knowledge, and authenticity.

WHY OVERCOMING SELF-LIMITING BELIEFS MATTERS

Self-limiting beliefs can come in an array of shapes and forms. Some beliefs have a cultural/family origin, whereas others may be religiously based.

Pay attention to your protégés' self-limiting or self-defeating beliefs, expressed in statements such as

- "I'm no good at math."
- "I can't write well."
- "I'm not good at anything."
- "I'm just not the corporate type."
- "Statistics is hard—I won't do well in this class."
- "You have to be really smart to be a . . . or do . . . I'm not that smart."
- "Girls can't be engineers."
- "Boys aren't dancers."
- "I got in because I was lucky."
- "Liberal arts isn't a useful major."
- "Only rich people get to do that."
- "People from my neighborhood/family don't do . . ."
- "People who work in corporations only care about money and are out for themselves only."
- "My racial/cultural group isn't good at . . ."
- "College is for "A" students only."
- "I won't get a scholarship because I don't have a 4.0 GPA."

In Chapter 17, I wrote about the mentor's role as a cheerleader, the builder of confidence, speaker of positive words. There is an important corollary to this role—the mentor also has to help the protégé overcome self-defeating or self-limiting beliefs.

When your protégé appears stuck, it is imperative that you have an understanding of any self-defeating beliefs in the way. Your job is to guide your protégé past any self-limitations so as to facilitate growth and development.

PRACTICAL STRATEGIES FOR HELPING PROTÉGÉS PAST SELF-LIMITING BELIEFS

You do not need to wrestle your protégés into changing beliefs, but can gently offer alternative viewpoints that will expand their views. You can even influence a protégé's beliefs in humorous ways, offering perspectives and ways of thinking through stories and jokes.

Consider these strategies for helping protégés overcome self-limiting beliefs:

- When helping a protégé with self-limiting beliefs, always keep in mind the end goal of mentoring: to promote the development and potential of the protégé.
- Be curious and ask questions about how they came to this belief.
- Ask about possible cultural, religious, or family influences that may have led to these beliefs.
- Invite them to discuss and examine their beliefs.
- Take the time to understand the protégé's beliefs before coming up with strategies or solutions.
- Take the time to figure out how protégés can honor their cultural/family values and succeed at the same time.
- Be respectful about their beliefs when offering alternative scenarios; for example, "I understand how you may believe . . . I'd like to offer another explanation though—what if you also gave yourself some credit for what you achieved?"
- Offer help and support when challenging beliefs; for example, "Let's get you some exposure to statistics. How about I'll show you some of the statistics I use in my research?" or "I know some women scientists who love their jobs. How about I introduce you to them?"
- Brainstorm strategies with your protégé when coming up with alternative perspectives and solutions.
- Remind protégés about their achievements when they are doubting themselves. Point out their strengths and accomplishments.

Part III

Facilitating the Protégé's Socialization

All protégés have to live, function, work, and play in a wide array of micro- and macro-environments, be it school, work, home, community groups, religious settings, college, or society as a whole.

Entering into any new environment can be extremely stressful, confusing, and frustrating, partly because protégés need to learn new skills and partly because learning the ropes is not a straightforward, explicit affair. In addition, the multiple worlds and identities of protégés can and will interface, influence each other, and even collide at times.

Mentors play a critical role in helping protégés integrate and interface successfully in all the environments they are in. With you by their side, your protégés can not only survive, but thrive even when challenges confront them.

The mentor strategies in this section are instrumental in helping your protégés negotiate multiple worlds. Most importantly, these strategies will help your protégés feel a sense of belonging and ownership in their various school, personal, and professional communities. This feeling of fitting in and being accepted is essential to their persevering and becoming successful. This section covers the following mentor strategies that help facilitate socialization:

- being proactive
- providing opportunities
- role-modeling
- providing access to the inside story
- endorsing
- building community
- protecting

Chapter 21

Being Proactive

Mentoring can be relatively passive if, say, one merely serves as a role model, but in the paradigm I label "the proactive mentor," the mode is more active and nurturing.

— J. Perez (1993, p. 40)

CASE EXAMPLE: A PROACTIVE MENTOR
CHANGES THE LIFE OF ONE INNER-CITY CHILD

Growing up in a large family, Tamika was an extremely shy kid whose voice was rarely heard.

In school, she struggled because she was too shy to ask questions. She tried to figure everything out by herself, but this strategy backfired on her, especially in her science and math classes. She started to believe she wasn't cut out for school.

A turning point came when she participated in a summer science camp for inner-city kids. The camp was an outreach program designed to introduce inner-city kids to the world of science through a rich array of fun activities, such as field trips to an actual crime lab, conducting cool science experiments, and meeting real scientists at work.

The program paired each kid with a mentor from the local Ivy League college. Tamika's mentor was Malik, a college sophomore majoring in genetics. Malik had a gift for sensing the needs of his students and reaching out to them. He intuitively understood Tamika's shyness and learning style, and took her aside for one-on-one tutorials where she could ask questions without fear of being made fun of. Each day, Tamika got the opportunity to ask him all kinds of questions on all manner of subjects. As a result, Malik sparked Tamika's interest in science, in going to college, and in becoming a biochemist.

After the summer camp was over, their mentoring relationship continued, through e-mails, text messages, and the occasional phone call or visit to Tamika's family. Tamika looked up to Malik as her big brother in science who was watching over her.

Malik watched carefully over her as she progressed through elementary school, then junior high, then high school. He never once said, "Call me anytime," and left it at that. Instead, he took the time to check in with her and asked her how she was doing. He also proactively told her about information she needed to know about science careers and college. He prepared her for all the steps she needed to take in order to get ready for college, such as how to get free SAT preparation, how to write the personal statement, how to get an early college acceptance, and how and when to apply for scholarships. He even arranged for Tamika to do a summer internship at a biotech company so she could get real-life exposure to biotech careers.

Reflecting on his mentoring of Tamika, Malik said: "I've had to figure out a lot in my life, and it's been frustrating. A lot of what I've learned, I've learned by screwing up the first time. I don't want Tamika to have to do that. I'm in a position where I know certain things. I figured it was my job to just pass them along and save her time."

Tamika eventually got admitted into her top-choice college with a full scholarship. She is deeply appreciative for his proactive mentoring: "I think what makes it mentoring is that he gets the steps of what needs to be done so I can stay on schedule. I don't know a lot of what needs to be done, but he keeps me on the ball. He'd say, 'You need to do this and you need to do that. Make sure you get this done. Let me see it to make sure that it's done right.' I didn't have to beg him for anything. I could tell that I'm on his mind because he would just tell me all these opportunities, like scholarships and the summer internship. To me, this is what makes it a mentoring relationship."

WHY BEING PROACTIVE MATTERS

Most people are absolutely sincere when they say—"Call me if you have any questions."

However, there's an inherent problem with this well-meaning statement— it is simply impossible for protégés to ask questions about topics they don't know about.

For instance, someone new to college would not know enough to ask about the significance of terms such as "credit/no credit," "withdrawal," and "transfer." International students unfamiliar with the customs of American schools would not even think to inquire about the support services available to them. Ethnic minority individuals who are the first in their families to go to college or enter a profession are likely to have huge gaps in their knowledge about school or work.

Since protégés are limited in what they know, they are likely to stumble, make lots of mistakes, waste a lot of time, and possibly get so discouraged that they give up.

This is why it is so vital that mentors be proactive about educating their protégés about how they can succeed and informing them about the resources available to them. Mentors play a critical and indispensable role in teaching protégés about resources, information, and opportunities they wouldn't otherwise know about.

It's great to invite your protégé to ask questions and to tell them that your door is open to them. But I invite you to take your mentoring to the next level by proactively giving information and answering the questions your protégé might *not* think of asking. Instead of waiting for them to ask questions, think about the questions they *should* be asking. Talk about these questions with them. Tell them information they should know but are not asking about. Figure out the gaps in their knowledge and fill in these holes for them.

For instance, if you are mentoring teachers in training, think about all the things they *don't* know and give them information in these areas, such as teachers' associations, conferences, and other support resources.

If you're mentoring future doctors, talk to them about career opportunities pre-med and beyond. Talk to them about the inside workings of being a doctor and about parts of the job they may not necessarily associate with being a doctor. Talk to them about how to make it smoothly through med school and residency.

Having a mentor means your protégés don't have to figure things out all by themselves. When you proactively watch out for your protégés, you are helping them maximize their strengths and potential, while minimizing obstacles. You are not only saving them time, but are shielding them from needless discouragement and frustration.

PRACTICAL STRATEGIES FOR BEING PROACTIVE

Don't wait for your protégés to ask before telling them things. Instead, think proactively about things they might not know. Make the effort to tell them about information, opportunities, or events that they would not find out on their own.

Here are some things you could proactively do with your protégé:

- Break down all the big and little steps needed to achieve a goal, such as how to get ready for high school, how to apply for college, and how to transfer to a four-year institution.
- Give them the big picture of what lies ahead—what you and they envision in their future after high school, college, in five years' time, and so forth.
- Tell them about opportunities that they may not have heard of, such as scholarships, training opportunities, grants, workshops, free classes, and so on.
- Discuss issues in their fields of interest, such as the opportunities for growth as well as the pitfalls.
- Brainstorm potential obstacles to their goals, and discuss ways to minimize or reduce obstacles before they occur.
- Give them the insider's perspective of what it is like to be in your profession.
- Give them useful information that can support their efforts. Pass on brochures, articles, resources, or good Web links that can help them.
- Invite them to join you in professional events or special projects.
- Introduce them to insiders in the field.

Chapter 22

Providing Opportunities

I was very fortunate to collaborate with the most brilliant choreographer, George Balanchine, who became my mentor in Ballet. I took advantage of this great opportunity, and we worked together to build the very successful New York City Ballet Company.

—Maria Tallchief, National Medal of Arts Winner (1999)

CASE EXAMPLE: A MENTOR PROACTIVELY PROVIDES OPPORTUNITIES

Rashid was a high school student who tried hard in his classes, but struggled constantly because of attention deficit disorder and dyslexia. He also lived in a tough neighborhood where gangs, drugs, and homicides were the norm. His mom was a single parent who worried constantly about Rashid's welfare. She hoped he would complete high school, but knew that the temptations of drug money might prevail.

A lucky break came when Rashid enrolled in the Culinary Academy, a specialty program offered by his high school. Culinary Academy was the one place on campus where Rashid shone. He loved prepping ingredients and transforming them into dishes that wowed his friends. Amidst the heat and bustle of the kitchen, he found focus doing the kitchen tasks he loved. He surprised himself with his level of concentration and precision.

Rashid's passion was nurtured and encouraged by his Culinary Academy teacher, Lavinia, a former chef who became a teacher after a back injury. She knew well the lure of gangs and drugs just beyond the borders of the school and kept a close eye on the students under her watch.

Lavinia was thrilled to have a student with Rashid's level of enthusiasm and commitment. In turn, she provided a wide variety of opportunities for him to develop his skills:

- She told him about a national cooking competition for high school students and encouraged him to enter his recipe for vegetarian lasagna. Rashid placed fourth and the experience bolstered his confidence and confirmed his passion for cooking.
- She told him about an internship at a high-end restaurant. This gave Rashid invaluable restaurant experience before he even started his junior year.
- She told him about a job at a bakery which fit his school hours and was within walking distance of the high school. In the bakery, Rashid learned the art of bread-making and made some much-needed money. Best of all, the bakery was a safe after-school refuge.
- She took him to a Food Expo, where he could meet experts and see different aspects of the food industry. There, Rashid got the idea of creating his own line of healthy salad dressings.

Lavinia also made available another incredible opportunity to Rashid when she told him about a scholarship to the prestigious Culinary Institute of America. Thanks to all the culinary experiences he gained through Lavinia, Rashid won the scholarship. He is now attending the CIA tuition-free and has dreams of becoming an executive chef someday.

Lavinia was an excellent teacher who taught Rashid the foundational skills he needed to know in the kitchen. However, she didn't stop at teaching him knife skills and baking secrets. She also showed him all the ins and outs of the trade and provided rich opportunities to nurture his growth and learning.

Rashid is grateful for how she opened up possibilities in his life: "She told me about so many great opportunities to advance my career. I am so far ahead of my friends because she looked out for me. I've seen other people just lose their way because no one guided them like Lavinia guided me. I wouldn't even have known about any of these opportunities, but she made the effort to tell me about them. This was a *big* deal for me. She opened up the world to me."

WHY PROVIDING OPPORTUNITIES MATTERS

Parents, teachers, and mentors who want to be encouraging might say: "Seize any opportunities that come your way! Don't be afraid to take advantage of opportunities!"

This is great advice. But an outstanding mentor goes beyond saying the right words. They *tell* their protégés when good career opportunities come up. They also *provide* opportunities.

The key to being an outstanding mentor is being *proactive*. Don't wait for your protégés to ask for things. Think about their needs and help them identify ways to enhance their lives with rich experiences. Pass on information about opportunities.

Your protégé is not likely to know about the opportunities out there, let alone ask for them. Ethnic minorities, in particular, might not feel comfortable asking you to provide opportunities for them. They might be too shy, be intimidated, or be afraid of sounding pushy. It's up to you, the mentor, to look out for them and open their eyes to the rich possibilities available to them.

PRACTICAL STRATEGIES FOR
PROVIDING OPPORTUNITIES

Start by paying attention to notices in newspapers, television, bulletin boards, the Internet, and anywhere information is posted. You will find all kinds of terrific opportunities that you can pass on to your protégés. Often, professional associations and community organizations offer scholarships, grants, unique learning opportunities, and terrific resources.

Be creative as you think about opportunities to enhance your protégés' development. One enterprising teacher organized a book reading at a local bookstore so her first-graders could read their stories in public. A protégé who wants to develop leadership skills can start a club in school or run for leadership positions in campus organizations.

Talk often with your protégés about their dreams and goals (see Chapter 15 on "Discussing Dreams and Goals"). Ask them how they'd like their resumes to look like in five, ten years. Discuss all the big and little steps they need to take in order to achieve those dreams. You might also suggest additional activities they can do to get a rich breadth of experiences.

Tell them about or provide the opportunities that will make this visualization a reality.

You can also provide enriching opportunities by inviting your protégés to join you in your projects.

IDEAS FOR PROVIDING OPPORTUNITIES

Here are some areas for providing opportunities to enhance your protégés' development.

Note that most of these are applicable to all age groups. Don't underestimate your protégé—a six-year-old might well be interested in writing,
publishing, public speaking or learning a new skill!

- any skill or subject (anything from architecture to oceanography, politics
  to zoology)
- camps
- public speaking opportunities
- leadership experiences (running for positions in school, work or in the
  community)
- writing and publishing
- managing money
- supervisory and management experience
- creative/artistic experiences, such as going to an art museum
- research
- workshops, classes, or conferences
- public/community service
- volunteering
- community organizing
- starting a club or group
- scholarships and grants
- contests, competitions, and recitals
- starting a business or nonprofit

Chapter 23

Role Modeling

Example is not the main thing in influencing others. It is the only thing.

—Albert Schweitzer (as cited in *Book of Positive Quotations*, 1993, p. 387)

CASE EXAMPLE: HOW ONE
MENTOR'S ROLE-MODELING TAUGHT
AND INSPIRED HIS PROTÉGÉ

Yoshiro is a third-generation Japanese American who came from a long line of successful business leaders in the hotel industry. His parents practically raised him in the boardroom, grooming him to be part of the family business.

Yoshiro spent fifteen years managing his family's hotel and knew all the tricks of the trade of the hotel industry. He was good at his job, but his heart was simply not in hotel management. Secretly, he dreamed of being an art teacher and an artist. But he did not have a clue as to how to make a career out of being an artist. Everyone around him was knowledgeable about business, but no one in his circle of friends and family had ever gone into fine arts.

What saved him was taking an art class with a talented water-colorist who had moved from corporate America into teaching. Yoshiro remembers feeling inspired and amazed on first meeting his teacher: "He was the first Asian American male art teacher I'd ever met. Seeing him in action, seeing him teach art, was incredible for me."

Yoshiro's teacher, Chin, became an incredible role model for him. Chin's very existence as an artist and art teacher served as motivation and inspiration for Yoshiro. Chin was also generous in sharing his professional life—he invited Yoshiro to accompany him to art exhibitions, sit in his classrooms, attend his public lectures, and visit his studio. Yoshiro was enthralled as he watched his mentor paint, give lectures, and teach art to adults and kids in settings as diverse as elementary schools, hospitals, and prisons.

Thanks to Chin's openness about his many different professional roles, Yoshiro had a greatly expanded knowledge of career possibilities in art. He realized he didn't have to be a starving artist, a fate that had worried his family to no end. He began to visualize his own niche and identity in the art world.

Yoshiro eventually got an art degree and married his disparate interests by producing as well as distributing fine art to boutique hotels. He also teaches art once a week at the local community college. Now he opens his students' eyes to the kaleidoscope of professional possibilities in art, just as his mentor did with him many years ago.

WHY ROLE MODELING MATTERS

Never underestimate the importance of observational learning.

Think about how a baby learns to talk—accomplishing this one skill involves constant listening, observing, and imitation of the speech of caregivers. It is magical when a baby utters that first word, but behind the magic is much practice and learning from caregiver role modeling.

Likewise, what your protégés learn from you can be deeply inspiring, informative, and life changing. They can learn a lot just by observing you at work and play.

An outstanding mentor is somebody who watches over the protégé. At the same time, outstanding mentors also allow their protégés to watch *them* work.

Role modeling is an especially critical mentor function if your protégés lack role models in their lives. Ethnic minority individuals, in particular, might be the first in their families to try a new professional role and are sorely in need of a caring role model. *You* might be the sole role model for them.

There is no need to feel pressure about being the "perfect" role model without any flaws or failures. You can think of yourself as being a realistic and holistic role model, showing your strengths and talents, but not hiding difficulties and challenges either. The point is not to role model perfection. Rather, the point is to role model enthusiasm, hard work, and willpower in action.

Instead of setting yourself up to impossible standards, simply show your protégé how you bring the best of your abilities to work and how you handle challenges and setbacks. Your protégés will learn as much from your successes as they will from how you handle your limitations.

PRACTICAL STRATEGIES FOR BEING AN EFFECTIVE ROLE MODEL

You can be an excellent role model simply by being open about your different professional roles and by giving your protégés opportunities to observe you in action. Break down the different components of your job and explain how you work. There's a lot that goes into a profession, whether you are a car mechanic, doctor, teacher, construction worker, Web designer, or college student. For instance, if you are a car mechanic, you could show your protégés how to speak with customers, how to balance books, how to write invoices, and how to tackle different auto problems.

You can also be an inspiring role model by showing your enthusiasm for your work. Likewise, your integrity in your work and personal life translates to role modeling in action. Keep the following in mind when you think about role modeling:

- Break down all the big and small components of your work as well as your protégé's work or school life, such as writing a book report, working on a team, chairing a meeting, speaking to customers, leading a group, writing documentation. Demonstrate and explain these components.
- Don't forget the basic essentials, such as how to address people, how to approach teachers and professors, how to write an e-mail, how to bill a customer.
- Tell stories about how you accomplished things in school, college or work—these stories can teach your protégés.
- Describe your enthusiasm for different parts of your job.
- Tell your protégé how you handle setbacks in work and life.
- Invite your protégé to watch you in action, such as giving a speech, teaching a class, working as a team-member, and so forth.
- Show how you balance your work role with other parts of your life, such as being a partner, parent, family member, student, member of a cultural, community or religious group, and so forth.

Chapter 24

Providing Access to the Inside Story

I realized that some [White] students understood things I didn't. They learned from their fraternities about how the power structure worked. They learned how to maneuver around the institution. I learned it the hard way because I didn't maneuver. I remember talking to one of my professors, I hadn't done well in his course, and he told me, "If I had known you were getting into trouble, you could have come to me and talked about it." I didn't know that. I didn't know that was part of the rules. . . . I realized that whatever explicit rules there are in the institution, there are also unspoken rules. Whatever objective criteria there are, there are also subjective criteria. So one of the tricks in an institution is to understand not only objective criteria, but also subjective criteria—not only the written rules, but also the unwritten rules.

—A Black executive (quoted in Thomas and Gabarro, 1999, p. 19).

CASE EXAMPLE: A MENTOR PROVIDES ACCESS TO THE INSIDE STORY OF HIGHER EDUCATION

Gracia Gomez's parents eked out a meager living in the strawberry fields of Watsonville, California. The Gomezes worked long hours, but struggled to put food on the table. They were loving, concerned parents who wanted the best for Gracia, but neither was familiar with the educational system in the United States and could give her guidance.

One day, Hortensia Diaz, a Puente[1] counselor from the local community college, visited Gracia's high school and explained the different paths to getting a four year college degree. She told them about the Puente program and how it supported students through community college and beyond.

Gracia's heart beat fast as Hortensia shared her story of attending community college and then transferring to a University of California campus. Gracia's single thought was "I want to be just like her!"

Their mentoring relationship blossomed after Gracia visited Hortensia at her community college campus. Hortensia showed her the campus, pointing out the different facilities and programs that Gracia could participate in. Throughout the visit, Gracia visibly glowed as she imagined being a member of this academic community.

The visit was enjoyable for both women—each instantly appreciated and respected the other's warmth, dynamism, and commitment to social justice. After the campus visit, they met regularly, often over a meal of enchiladas (Gracia's favorite dish) or *agua fresca* (a traditional Mexican fruit beverage). As was customary in their shared culture, Marina got to know Gracia's family and was warmly included in all their family celebrations, like the confirmation and *quinceañera* (the fifteenth birthday celebration) of her sister.

In turn, Marina was Gracia's guide to community college and higher education, a world that was initially mysterious to Gracia and her parents. Marina explained how to prepare for college, encouraging Gracia to take advanced placement classes in the subjects she was good at. Marina also demystified college for Gracia, telling her the unwritten protocols about college that can make, break, or accelerate a student's success. She told her about invaluable support resources that Gracia didn't know about, like scholarships for high school students, work study jobs, and special classes for the Puente program.

Gracia is quick to acknowledge how much Marina has taught her: "Marina told me things I didn't know and wouldn't have found out by myself. I wouldn't even have known about community college! My parents didn't know these things either. I would have been completely lost without her. I wouldn't have been able to achieve all the things I have done if not for her. She's my *angél de la guarda* [guardian angel]."

After high school, Gracia made a completely smooth transition into community college—quite a feat considering she didn't even know about the existence of community college two years prior.

Since enrolling in community college, Gracia has blossomed, surpassing even her own dreams and expectations for herself. She has been earning good grades and contributing to the college through her leadership of student organizations like Mecha and student government. Notes Hortensia, "She is an integral part of our campus. She really brings something special to our community."

Currently, Gracia is working toward transferring to a four-year institution to fulfill her dreams of becoming a doctor. Her mentoring relationship with

Hortensia is stronger than ever. They see each other at least three times a week. Gracia often pops into Hortensia's office to say "Hi," or Hortensia might invite Gracia for a coffee break at the campus café. As she did from the beginning of their relationship, Hortensia keeps a close watch on Gracia's progress and gives a continual stream of advice and inside tips so she has full access to opportunities in higher education.

WHY TELLING THE INSIDE STORY MATTERS

Every institution, organization, and field has its written and unwritten rules. The unwritten rules—the inside information known only to insiders—constitute what I call the "inside story."

The unwritten rules may be unpublished and unspoken, but they are every bit as important as the written rules.

Knowing and abiding by these unwritten rules can be essential for smooth sailing through school and work. Those in the know are well aware of the rules of the inside story and can navigate easily through the system.

On the other hand, being unaware of or breaking unwritten rules could damage one's career. For example, I know of one psychology graduate program that frowns on students who delay their comps (doctoral exams) or ask for time off. Nowhere is it written explicitly that students should take their comps on time and not take vacations during the semester. Yet, there are consequences to breaking these unwritten rules.

Outsiders tend to be shut out from the inside story, and tend to be unaware of the unwritten rules. Consequently, they have a much tougher time making it through the system. One graduate student I talked to did not know the unwritten rule that grades are considered less important than research in her doctoral program. As a result, she spent too much time preparing for classes when she should have focused more on her research.

Noted one mentor: "From birth through adulthood, most successful white males in America have had access to informal guidance, tutoring, and coaching from older male sponsors, social club directors, recreation directors and community leaders. Upper-middle class white males like the Kennedys, the Rockefellers, and the Bushes have been guided through prep schools and prestigious colleges to make the right connections to facilitate success in school and entry into the professions, academia, politics, and, in general, leadership roles. Women and ethnic minorities have traditionally not had access to these informal mentors to teach them the inside story. Hence, they spend an undue amount of time going down blind alleys and making uninformed choices despite outstanding ability and academic preparation. When minorities and women don't succeed to the level of their potential, is it because they lack the right stuff or because they did not have effective mentoring, guidance and coaching from senior respected figures in the professional community?"

PRACTICAL STRATEGIES: HOW MENTORS CAN TELL THE INSIDE STORY

Mentors play a critical role in helping protégés understand and access the inside story. By explaining and teaching the unwritten rules, you will open the doors for your protégés to take full advantage of school, work, and community resources and opportunities. Your mentoring will also help them avoid potential problems and pitfalls that might otherwise derail them.

It is never too early to teach your protégé about the inside story. Even a kindergarten gets the concept of unwritten rules in the school and playground. A student in high school could likewise benefit from understanding how best to apply for coveted spots, such as a student council position or college. An early career professional needs to know how to move up the career ladder.

It is key to be *proactive* in telling the inside story—protégés need you to take charge since they are likely to be unaware of inside secrets. Don't wait for them to ask you—they are unlikely to know about the inside story and are even less likely to ask about unwritten rules.

Start by reflecting on the written and unwritten rules that are vital for your protégé to know. Then offer access to the inside story in the following ways:

- Talk frequently about the issues, the dos and don'ts, customs, and unwritten rules of schools, work places, and professions.
- Give information on hidden opportunities (such as funding opportunities, scholarships, contests, and publishing opportunities).
- Discuss resources, associations, groups, and organizations to join that will benefit your protégé, such as the American Association of University Women, Puente program for college-bound students, Big Brothers Big Sisters for younger protégés, small business associations for entrepreneurs, and so forth.
- Tell your protégé about educational and career enhancement opportunities like job training programs, community college, adult education, and continuing education classes.
- Discuss opportunities that can broaden your protégé's horizons, such as participation in student or professional organizations.
- Provide information on different types of careers.

- Discuss the professional field and different subspecialties and niches.
- Talk about the latest advances in the field and the people spearheading these trends.
- Discuss the proper way to format a resume or curriculum vitae.
- Discuss strategies for applying for jobs, promotions, schools, college, or graduate school.
- Discuss the dos and don'ts when interviewing for a scholarship, job, or position.
- Tell them how they can advance smoothly and quickly in their careers.

Above all, give your protégé as much guidance and information as possible so they can make decisions and choices that are fully informed and can have full access to school and career opportunities.

NOTE

1. Puente is an academic preparation and support program in California that assists educationally disadvantaged students enter college.

.

Chapter 25

Endorsing

Bob Stone (his English teacher) wrote the director (of a graduate program in drama) a letter that basically said, "If you don't have the talent to nurture this young man, then don't accept him." . . . That letter of recommendation was a big deal, which is why I still carry it with me. . . . I must have reread that letter a hundred times . . . To have someone believe in you that much is a tremendous boost. It left me thinking, "Well something's going on here. I better pay attention to it, and nurture it, and see it through. . . . he gave me something to live up to. He lit a fire in me.

—Denzel Washington, actor, (Washington and Paisner, 2006, p. 18)

CASE EXAMPLES: HOW TWO MENTORS ENDORSED THEIR PROTÉGÉS AND PAVED THEIR WAY TO SUCCESS

A mentor's endorsement is like having a Good Housekeeping seal of approval. Here are two stories of how mentors helped their protégés with their endorsements.

CASE EXAMPLE #1

Latasha, a high school senior, was applying to colleges nationwide. Her top choice was a historically Black college whose academic environment would be a perfect fit for her. Latasha's mentor, her math teacher, happened to be a graduate of the college and was on a first-name basis with the faculty there. He wrote a three-page letter of recommendation that detailed his in-depth knowledge of Latasha's strengths, her accomplishments, how she had overcome multiple hardships, and his high regard of her potential. It was a standout letter that showcased the mentor's depth of knowledge and regard for Latasha.

Amazing as the letter was, Latasha's mentor went one step further and contacted a faculty friend at the college, personally vouching for Latasha's excellence as a student and person. Latasha's good grades, together with her superb letters of recommendation and the personal endorsement from her mentor, not only earned her a spot in the college of her dreams, but a full-ride scholarship as well.

CASE EXAMPLE #2

Joshua, a graduate student in teacher education, had a special passion for teaching Deaf children. However, none of his training sites offered him access to this population. Joshua's mentor made a personal call to a friend who was a teacher at a local Deaf school. This one phone call opened up the opportunity for Joshua to be a teaching aide in the teacher's classroom. Joshua loved the school, the students, and the staff—and the feeling was warmly reciprocated. When Joshua earned his teaching credential, he was hired to be a full-time teacher at the school.

WHY ENDORSING MATTERS

Endorsing protégés simply means putting in a good word, either in-person, or via phone, e-mail, or letter. There is tremendous benefit to having a mentor's endorsement—it can open doors that would otherwise remain closed. It can unearth priceless career opportunities that might not otherwise be available to the protégé. It can smooth the way for the protégé to be admitted into a school or company.

Women, ethnic minorities, first-generation students, workers, and those from disadvantaged backgrounds often lack access to closed networks. Hence, the endorsement of mentors is especially critical for these groups.

PRACTICAL STRATEGIES FOR ENDORSING PROTÉGÉS OF ANY AGE

- Write letters of recommendation that are both personal and detailed. Be sure that you provide lots of specifics of your knowledge of your protégés, their strengths, and their abilities. A detailed, personalized letter is a thousand times more effective than a generic one.

- If your protégé is applying for college, a position, grant, or other opportunity, make a personal call or write an e-mail to the decision-makers if possible. This extra step adds a powerful, personal touch to your recommendation.
- Introduce your protégé to people who can help advance their skills or careers, such as teachers, coaches, colleagues, friends, and professors.
- Formally and/or informally nominate your protégé for opportunities, such as community, work, and school projects, scholarships, awards, research projects, or work assignments.

Chapter 26

Building Community

I say it takes a tribe to raise a child. You have to have people who are interacting with each other to raise a child, people who are connected to that child. . . . If you don't have this tribe or this pack or this pride to pass on accumulated wisdom and experience, where does the child get it? You have to get it from somewhere. If you don't get it from family and tribe, you're going to get it from the street, and that usually means from the worst influences on the street.

—Gen. Colin Powell (ashington and Paisner, 2006, p. 181)

CASE EXAMPLE: HOW ONE MENTOR HELPED HER PROTÉGÉ BE A PART OF A PROFESSIONAL COMMUNITY

Growing up in a middle-class Mexican American family, Ricardo loved watching television with his family. They would gather together on the couch in the evenings, often commenting on the presence (or absence) of Mexican Americans on national TV. These conversations inspired Ricardo's dream of becoming a news anchor on TV.

Ricardo took all the right steps to ensure a successful career in journalism—he worked hard in high school, was accepted into a college with a strong journalism program, earned good grades, and excelled in his internship at the college newspaper. All these steps were critical, but his career really took off when he found a mentor in Marisa Nunez, a respected radio journalist who herself had helped blaze the trail for Hispanic news journalists.

Knowing how isolating it was to be an ethnic minority in this profession, Marisa was conscientious about helping Ricardo feel a part of a professional community. She did this by introducing him to many ethnic minorities as well as European American broadcasters and journalists. These were people with established careers who got to know him, took him under their wings, made him feel like he belonged to a big family, and even offered him jobs. Marisa also introduced Ricardo to people who were just starting out. These peers formed another source of support and community for him.

Marisa had this to say about her intentions in making these introductions: "It's helpful for Ricardo to meet the leaders in broadcasting who are good friends of mine. The point is not for him to rub shoulders with famous people but to give him the opportunity to meet people he wouldn't otherwise get to know, people who can actually help him and who have some common interests with him."

Ricardo noted that he felt like a "nobody" until Marisa came along. Said Ricardo, "A big thing she did was to introduce me to people. But she didn't introduce me in a superficial way. She didn't just say, 'Ricardo, meet so-and-so.' She would say: 'I'm going to meet my friends for coffee. Why don't you join me?' And so it became a meaningful interaction because I got to know a lot of people as friends of Marisa's."

When I asked Ricardo to explain why these introductions were so important to him, he replied: "Because those circles don't open. It's just not easy to meet people that are established. By introducing me in such a personal way, she opened her network to me. And that was really influential in making me feel like a professional."

WHY BUILDING COMMUNITY MATTERS

Research has shown that students who feel engaged and have a sense of belonging to a community tend to persist and succeed better than those who are isolated. This finding makes sense. But the tough part is creating a sense of community for students, workers, and protégés who are new to the school or work environment and have limited access to closed networks.

As a mentor, you play a vital role in helping your protégés integrate successfully into their school and work communities. By introducing them to different people in these communities, you are playing a critical role in helping them feel like part of a professional family. You are helping them feel a sense of belonging.

You can introduce your protégé to the leaders, movers, and shakers of the field.

You can also introduce them to their peers in the field and to upcoming fresh blood.

Help your protégé get to know wonderful people who share their professional interests and passions.

Help them create a circle and community of people whom they can count on.

The point of these introductions is not to rub shoulders with famous people or to make your protégé the life of the party. Rather, the goal is pure and simple—to help your protégés feel a sense of family and kinship within the vast, bewildering environments of the school, field, or profession they are in. This is especially important for ethnic minority protégés entering into a predominantly European American world—helping them be a part of a community will give them a sense of belonging that will support their persistence and aid in their success.

PRACTICAL STRATEGIES FOR HELPING YOUR PROTÉGÉS BUILD COMMUNITY

Here are the different ways to build your protégés' connections and community:

- Before making introductions, discuss with your protégés how to interact with different people in their schools or professional communities. For instance, protégés new to college need to be coached on the "etiquette" of approaching professors.
- Introduce your protégés to more experienced colleagues as well as peers who share similar professional and personal interests or cultural/family/racial backgrounds.
- Make introductions via e-mail, phone, or in person.
- When making introductions, describe your protégé's background, skills, and talents. Explain why you are connecting them together and how they can benefit each other.
- When making an e-mail introduction, write a personal e-mail to introduce your protégé. Giving your personal touch to an e-mail introduction helps solidify the introduction.
- Invite your protégé to accompany you to events or meetings where they can meet other professionals and colleagues.
- Take your protégés out for meals or coffee with other people, thus allowing them to get to know each other in a more informal, relaxed setting.

Chapter 27

Protecting

"You went alone!" Haji Ali accused him. "You didn't seek the hospitality of a village chief! If you learn only one thing from me, learn this lesson well: Never go anywhere in Pakistan alone. Promise me that."

—Mortenson and Relin (2006, p. 177)[1]

CASE EXAMPLE: A MENTOR'S PROTECTION SAVES THE DAY

Sewati grew up on an Indian reservation but opted to enroll in a community college to get a taste of life outside the reservation. Inspired by President Obama, Sewati hoped to become a lawyer and a community activist to help his tribe. As he packed his belongings, he reveled in big dreams for his future and his tribe.

However, he ran into an almost insurmountable roadblock on the very first day of his "History of European Civilizations" course, a prerequisite for legal studies majors. The class had barely begun when the instructor made a joke about ethnic minorities. Sewati scanned the classroom, wondering if anyone else noticed. No one reacted.

Interestingly, the only other ethnic minority student in the class did not return after the first class session. Sewati did not have this option since the course was a requirement for his major.

Sewati felt more and more uncomfortable as the class progressed and the instructor made increasingly derogatory comments about Native Americans and other ethnic groups. When Sewati politely questioned the instructor about one such comment, the instructor yelled at Sewati for being

125

"ignorant," and "disrespectful." Sewati stood his ground, but was quaking inside.

After the class, Sewati took refuge under a towering oak tree. His hands were trembling as he struggled to compose himself. As he watched the other students laughing without a care in the world, he noticed, with mounting anger, the college mascot (a cartoon of an Indian chief) emblazoned everywhere—on backpacks, sweatshirts, campus buildings, and even on the backside of a student's shorts.

Sewati questioned if he could continue in an institution that made such casual use of his culture's leaders. He contemplated returning home to the reservation. At the same time, he couldn't bear the thought of giving up his dream of getting his college degree.

Sewati's distress struck Dr. Hermione Perez, the college ombudsman, who happened to be walking by. She stopped to ask if he were okay. Her unexpected concern encouraged Sewati to disclose what just happened.

Sewati did not know that he was speaking to the premier advocate on the college campus. He had no expectation that anything would come out of their conversation beneath the oak tree. However, instead of leaving Sewati to his own devices, Dr. Perez spoke personally to the History Department chair, who arranged for a meeting to resolve the conflict.

Dr. Perez volunteered to accompany Sewati to the meeting. Sewati was grateful for her presence, especially when the instructor started getting heated and accused him of being a disruptive student who did not do his assignments. Sewati easily countered this unfounded accusation, thanks to Dr. Perez who had prepared him for the meeting beforehand and had advised him to bring all the assignments he had completed.

The meeting ended with the instructor holding firm to his contention that Sewati was a problem student. Debriefing after the meeting, Dr. Perez and Sewati agreed that it would be pointless and even detrimental for him to continue with this instructor. She came up with the idea that he complete the course through an independent study with another instructor. This was an alternative that would never have occurred to Sewati.

Thanks to Dr. Perez's protection and help, Sewati was able to complete his prerequisite course without having to suffer further harassment.

Despite his unpromising start, Sewati persevered and eventually found a place for himself in the college. He is now president of the Native American Students Association and is actively campaigning to change the college mascot.

The unusual first meeting between Sewati and Dr. Perez blossomed into a meaningful mentoring relationship for both. Said Sewati of the painful experience: "If I didn't have her support and have her on my side, I don't know what I would have done because it was so bad that I wanted to leave. It made all the difference in my life that she took the time to express her concern that day."

PROTECTING: WHY IT MATTERS AND WHEN IT'S NEEDED

A typical mentoring relationship may progress for years without the mentor ever having to protect the protégé. However, on the rare occasion, unfair, discriminatory, or illegal situations might cause serious damage to the protégé. Should such a situation occur, the mentor can offer support and guidance, and if appropriate, protection and advocacy.

Without a mentor, students and employees are likely to feel lonely and defenseless when they are most in need of protection. Having a mentor means having access to guidance, advice, and advocacy. It means not having to fend helplessly for oneself.

Protection does not mean that you immediately rush to save your protégé at the slightest hint of trouble. Instead, remember that the overall goal of mentoring is *not* to create dependency, but rather to empower your protégés and support the building of their personal and professional skills. Learning how to handle tricky situations is a critical skill to have in one's tool-kit. Don't deprive your protégés of learning this skill if they are capable of learning how to handle difficult situations themselves.

Though protection is important when appropriate, it should not be the dominant feature of your mentoring relationship. If your mentorship feels too much like a never-ending rescue mission, step back and examine what's going on from your end, your protégé, and the surrounding environment. Do an honest assessment as you ask yourself these questions:

• Who or what is the root cause(s) of my protégé's problems?
• Am I taking on too much responsibility for my protégé's welfare?
• What is hindering my protégé's ability to take charge of the situation?

TWO FORMS OF PROTECTION

You can protect your protégés in two ways—indirectly and directly:

Indirect Protection

Watch out for your protégés and step in with guidance and advice when they seem to be heading in a wrong direction. By doing so, you will be protecting them by helping them circumvent problems.

Be proactive about discussing potential problems and how to avoid trouble. Go over the list of potential problems they may encounter (see below "Possible Areas for Protection") and discuss how to sidestep problem areas.

Direct Protection

Direct protection might be appropriate when it is clear protégés can't and shouldn't handle challenges by themselves. You can provide direct protection by talking directly with the parties involved or to authority figures who can take appropriate action.

Before intervening, ask yourself if the situation requires you to step in or if your protégés can be coached to handle the situation themselves. Be sure to have a clear understanding of the situation before intervening. If your protégés are at fault, you would want them to take responsibility for their actions rather than shield them.

Discuss with your protégés how they might be able to handle the problem. If the situation warrants for your protégés to handle the situation themselves, then provide coaching, guidance, and support, rather than jumping in yourself.

POSSIBLE AREAS FOR PROTECTION

Protégés, regardless of age, may be vulnerable and need protection in the following areas. Harassment may be physical, sexual, emotional, or verbal and can be based on a wide variety of factors, including:

- sexual orientation (note: gay/transgender/lesbian/bisexual youth are particularly vulnerable in this regard)
- race, ethnicity, culture, background, socioeconomic status (e.g., being bullied or discriminated against because of one's race)
- religion (e.g., Sikhs, Muslims, Hindus, and Jews being targeted for their religion)
- gender (e.g., women and girls enduring derogatory comments in school or at the workplace)
- age (e.g., an employee who is discriminated because of her age)
- national origin (e.g., someone from Iraq who is labeled a terrorist)
- disability (whether mental or physical)

Watch out for the following issues that may be potential stumbling blocks for specific groups and might warrant your protection:

SCHOOL-AGED KIDS

- bullies
- pressures to conform
- problems with peers or teachers

- pressure to do drugs, drink, be sexually active, or commit crimes
- pressures to join gangs
- lack of safety in school or at home
- parental/family problems (such as poverty, drug, or alcohol use by parents)

COLLEGE STUDENTS

- problems at work, or from family, school, or community
- problems with professors, committees, or advisors
- pressure to abuse drugs or alcohol
- difficulties with peers
- problems with supervisors

TEACHERS IN TRAINING

- problems with students, fellow teachers, parents or administrators

WORKPLACE PROTÉGÉS

- problems with supervisors, colleagues, or supervisees
- pressures to take on too many work assignments
- unfair policies
- pressure to take on too much
- fallout from failed projects.

NOTE

1. Mortenson is a humanitarian who has built schools in remote regions of Pakistan and parts of Central Asia. Haji Ali was a village chief who mentored him when he first started his mission.

Part IV

Institutions and Mentoring

Chapter 28

What Institutions Can Do to Support Outstanding Mentoring

> I'd attended three large, predominantly white, universities and had never had a classmate or professor of color. While I did everything I could to fit in—to be one of the crowd, to avoid appearing like I had a chip on my shoulder—on the inside, I was dying of loneliness and a chronic sense of otherness. No matter where I was—the classroom, the dormitory, or just chillin' on campus—I was painfully and acutely aware that I was other.
>
> —Hardy (2009, p. 49)

BENEFITS OF MENTORING TO INSTITUTIONS

Without question, organizations and institutions reap benefits from mentoring in a variety of ways. Here is a partial list of the many benefits organizations enjoy from mentoring:

- better recruitment of employees and students (including people of color)
- better retention of employees and students (including people of color)
- increased persistence of employees and students
- increased commitment of employees and students to the organization or school
- better overall student and employee success
- higher GPAs in mentored students
- better job performance in mentored workers
- better rates of graduation
- higher levels of employee and student engagement with the institution
- greater productivity

- easier socialization of employees and students into the organization
- higher employee and student satisfaction with the organization
- reduced turnover of staff
- greater loyalty and commitment in both current staff and alumni

As you can see from the above list, protégés are not the only ones who benefit from mentoring. There is a ripple effect of benefits from the protégés to the organization when outstanding mentoring happens:

From the start to the end of the mentored individual's stay, the school or organization reaps multiple benefits. New employees and students who are mentored are able to hit the ground running as opposed to floundering and struggling to learn the ropes, thus saving the organization time and resources that would be otherwise spent in orientation and training.

Further, mentored students and employees are more productive and experience higher satisfaction during their stay in the organization. They have greater loyalty and commitment to the organization. Not only are they more likely to remain in the school/organization and be more productive contributors, they are also more likely to increase the talent pool by mentoring others and by recruiting similar-minded individuals. Their word-of-mouth endorsement and commitment to mentoring helps the organization develop a sought-after reputation for being an exceptional place to work or study.

As an added bonus, mentors themselves benefit from doing mentoring *and* these benefits are likewise enjoyed by organizations. These benefits include a greater commitment and enthusiasm of mentors for their work, careers, and the organizations they work in.

MENTORING: AN ANSWER TO RECRUITING DIVERSE STUDENTS AND EMPLOYEES

The long list of well-documented mentoring benefits points to a powerful antidote for institutions, corporations, and groups grappling with issues of recruitment and retention of students, volunteers, and employees, particular those of minority status and diverse backgrounds.

There is an answer to this diversity challenge—*quality mentoring relationships involving mentors knowledgeable about working with minority protégés.*

Institutions that are standouts at attracting minority recruits already know this secret. Mentoring is a distinguishing feature of institutional cultures that are successful at recruiting and retaining the best and brightest. In fact, one study of psychology programs successful at recruiting and retaining graduate students of color found that 82 percent of the departments studied had established mentoring systems (Rogers & Molina, 2006). If you are the head of an organization, department, school, or program wanting to attract and retain quality staff and students, you simply cannot ignore the importance of having a mentoring culture.

Think about it—imagine a top student or employee considering identical offers from two competing companies/schools. The only difference between the two is that one is noted for its warm mentoring culture. Which institution do you think would stand a better chance of recruiting the potential student or employee? Which institution is more likely to retain the individual over the long run?

Mentoring is a means of sharply distinguishing one school or organization from similar others. Having a true mentoring culture transforms the school and workplace climate. Instead of being impersonal, uncaring, and chilly institutions where people barely know each other, organizations with strong mentoring programs become warm, welcoming places that encourage productivity, engagement, and generativity.

With mentoring comes all the organizational benefits outlined above, including the added bonus of mentors and protégés who are emotionally invested in each other, in the work, and in the organization.

Some may object that mentoring takes time and energy. These critics are right . . . to an extent. Yes, it does take time to do quality mentoring. However, the benefits accrued far outweigh the investment of time and effort. In fact, compared to the prohibitive costs of constantly recruiting, training, then losing students and employees, it is relatively inexpensive to implement and maintain a quality mentoring program and provide support for ongoing mentoring pairs.

THE SECRET TO CREATING AND MAINTAINING A MENTORING CLIMATE IN AN INSTITUTION OR ORGANIZATION

The previous chapters have stressed the importance of the mentor being intentional and proactive when mentoring.

Likewise, there are specific and practical strategies *institutions* can employ to create and sustain a climate of mentoring.

These strategies can be summed up neatly with the acronym SECRET, which stands for Support, Education, Community, Reward, Evaluation, and Training.

Implementing these strategies will lay the foundation for a healthy and friendly work or school climate where mentoring relationships can form and flourish:

Support:

- Set aside funds for a mentoring coordinator and support staff to run a mentoring program and associated activities.
- Provide ongoing support for mentor-protégé pairs—such as a hotline, blog, or online group for discussing questions, problems, or concerns in the relationship.
- Provide ongoing support for mentors, such as one-on-one training, mentoring guides such as this book, or regular workshops on mentoring. Be sure to furnish incentives as well as time and room for mentors to attend these workshops, for example, a workshop with lunch provided.
- Provide material support for mentors to help their protégés, such as a small stipend to spend toward supplies for protégés, gift cards for mentors to encourage them to take their protégés out to coffee, or gift certificates to help mentors get supplies for protégés.
- Make time in the workweek for mentoring—allow mentors time and space to devote to mentoring
- Provide opportunities for mentoring pairs to meet each other, for example, through networking luncheons and talks by experts on selected career topics.
- Mentor the new mentor—be sure to offer extra support and follow-up for new mentors who might have questions or concerns when they start mentoring. One way to do this is to pair mentors with more seasoned mentors who can guide and support their mentoring efforts.
- Model support for cross-cultural mentoring by encouraging senior management to take on protégés from different cultural backgrounds.
- Show support for cross-cultural understanding by featuring speakers and workshop topics on issues of race and culture.

Education-educate all members of the organization (from groundskeeper to CEO) about mentoring:

- Educate everyone in the organization about mentoring and what it means. Education should be ongoing and start from the moment someone enters the organization. Education efforts should include one-on-one training, workshops, and freely available resources such as mentoring guides.
- Highlight mentoring in the organization's Website and literature, and explain the role of mentoring in the organization.
- Include mentoring as a regular feature or column in the company's newsletter.
- Include mentoring as part of normal workday or schoolday conversation. If mentoring is mentioned as much as "safety" or "standards," it becomes

normalized and integrated into the workplace. The heads of organizations and schools can do much to promote mentoring by mentioning it often, either with personal reference to their own mentors or to the mentoring opportunities available within the organization.

- Educate mentors and protégés about racial, cultural, and diversity concerns.
- Invite speakers to talk about mentoring.

Community—create a sense of a mentoring community:

- Create a well-designed mentoring program that includes everyone in the organization from the newest employee to the person with the most authority.
- Make it a norm that every individual in the organization is a protégé and has a mentor. Everyone should be able to answer these two questions: "Who is your mentor?" and "Who is your protégé?"
- Host mentoring lunches, get-togethers, and socials so as to support and celebrate the mentoring community in your organization.
- Create an even larger sense of community and collaboration by partnering with other mentoring-friendly organizations, such as Big Brothers and Big Sisters.

Reward:

- Set up rewards for outstanding mentoring, such as public awards and special benefits. An inexpensive way to recognize mentoring efforts would be to post photos and biographies of the "Mentors and Protégés of the Month" in high-traffic areas. Another powerful and cost-effective incentive would be to designate a special parking spot for outstanding mentors.
- Give rewards for active participation in mentoring and mentoring-affiliated programs, for example, designating five-, ten-, and fifteen-year mentoring awards.
- Provide rewards and incentives for efforts to start or improve mentoring initiatives.
- Provide occasions for acknowledging and recognizing outstanding mentoring efforts, for example, awards ceremonies where protégés can thank mentors for their work, mentoring luncheons, and so forth.

Evaluation:

- Implement regular evaluations of mentoring programs and the effectiveness of mentor and protégé pairs.
- Have periodic but regular reviews of mentoring efforts within departments and the organization as a whole.

- Include mentoring as an evaluation criteria for mentors, protégés, and all staff. For instance, a company could include mentoring effectiveness in its work evaluation of employees. Schools and universities can include mentoring effectiveness in its evaluation of teachers, professors, and staff. Universities can include mentoring as a criterion for tenure.
- Include mentoring as a criterion in hiring interviews—ask potential candidates about their experiences as mentors and protégés. This will set the tone from the outset of the candidate's entry into the organization.

Training:

- Train mentors and protégés on how they can be outstanding mentors and protégés. This kind of training is indispensable prior to the beginning of the relationships. Hire a mentoring expert to teach all mentors about how to mentor and how to interact successfully with someone from a different background.
- Provide ongoing training on developing cross-cultural knowledge and skills.
- Provide opportunities for staff to participate in mentoring conferences (such as the International Mentoring Association annual conference) to update their mentoring skills and knowledge.

CASE EXAMPLE: USING THE SECRET
TO DIVERSIFY STUDENTS AND STAFF

A private school wishing to diversify its student pool could employ SECRET elements to increase its diversity pool. First, the school shores up support for existing internal diversity efforts by creating a mentoring program for all its students and staff. Each student and all new teachers are paired up with a mentor. The principal herself takes on two graduate student protégés—both of whom are people of color.

A consultant is hired to train mentors in effective cross-cultural mentoring practices. The school administration provides additional support for mentors by setting aside time each week for mentors to meet and discuss issues.

The establishment of strong mentoring relationships helps ensure retention of ethnic minority staff and students. The school climate changes with new conversations about mentoring successes and efforts.

The principal organizes a secret ballot twice a semester where students and staff can vote for their favorite mentors. The top three winners are publicly honored, with moving speeches by their protégés.

The school takes the additional step of educating students about mentoring and multiculturalism by infusing mentoring and diversity topics into the school's curriculum. Mentoring is celebrated and highlighted on "World Kindness Day."

Second, the school goes beyond school boundaries and reaches out to communities and agencies, partnering with these groups on community improvement projects, like cleaning up the local creek, planting vegetables in the community garden, and feeding the homeless.

The school invites the community in for school concert days and free workshops. Mentoring is prominently featured in these outreach efforts—potential students are warmly invited to be part of the mentoring program of the school. These outreach efforts result in the school becoming tightly woven into the fabric of the community. Diverse members of the community are now aware and appreciative of the school's presence and participation. The school thus establishes its reputation as being truly welcoming of diverse students and community participation.

Third, the school encourages its teachers, administrators, parents and students to initiate mentoring relationships with individuals outside the school. Gradually, tight mentoring relationships are formed to link the school and surrounding community organizations and professionals. In very little time, the private school not only dramatically improves its retention of minorities, it also easily recruits ethnic minorities because it has become known and respected for being truly inclusive and appreciative of multicultural concern.

As you can see from the above case example, mentoring relationships do not happen in a vacuum. They take place within the contexts of schools, communities, workplaces, colleges, and community agencies.

There's a lot that institutions can do to support and encourage quality mentoring relationships. Conversely, without institutional support for mentoring, there is far less possibility for mentoring relationships to flourish . . . and for the institution to reap benefits from mentoring.

If your corporation or school is struggling to recruit diverse individuals, don't miss out on a powerful tool to attract the best and brightest— effective cross-cultural mentoring. Often, the promise of mentors who will truly watch over, support, and guide protégés to higher levels of career advancement is an irresistible one that potential recruits will not easily refuse.

Chapter 29

Conclusion

> Now ask yourself: Who will carry *your* voice?. . . . Years from now, who in the world will receive your signal?. . . . Whether we mean to or not, we all leave a legacy. And the legacy that matters most is measured not in steel or silver or bone or blood. It is measured in the voice we pass on, a voice, disembodied, that can turn anything—a cockpit, some headphones, the heavens themselves—into a classroom. Look around. Right now, this very day, you are sending someone aloft.
>
> —Eric Liu (2004, p. 215)

I'm not lying when I say that writing my dissertation was pure joy from beginning to end. I know this sounds unbelievable, but it's the absolute truth. Part of the reason why the process was enjoyable rather than traumatic was because I had a solid core of mentors who supported me, cheered me on, and inspired me to do my best work. Best of all, my dissertation topic gave me the chance to witness extraordinary mentoring relationships that demonstrated the possibilities in human connection, kindness, and support.

As I listened to my research participants, I was impressed by the efforts and the amount of time they invested in their relationships. In an age of fast-paced technology where so much seems disposable and easily disregarded, where speed dating and instant messaging have become some of our norms for communicating and relating, it was truly refreshing to hear my participants referring to their mentoring relationships as "forever" relationships. Clearly, these were deeply meaningful relationships that mattered and were likely to endure.

Although it is certainly possible to have a mentoring "moment" where one stranger makes a difference in the life of another, these moments are not the same as the relationships I studied in my research. The latter demonstrate that quality long-term mentoring involves real relationships with real people, with a real commitment of time and effort.

Of course, there is the understandable objection that mentoring might take time away from the mentor's productivity and responsibilities. Certainly, quality mentoring takes time, but it's time worth spending given the multiple benefits enjoyed by protégés, mentors, as well as the institutions they are in.

To reap the benefits of mentoring, institutions must recognize, make allowances, and provide tangible support for the fact that quality mentoring demands skill, expertise, and commitment. This is particularly the case in mentoring relationships where opposites might not initially attract. Mentors who are ill-equipped to handle racial and cultural differences can innocently run their relationships down a rocky path riddled with missteps of divisive, sometimes destructive misunderstanding.

The good news is that the mentors and protégés I interviewed prove that even stark differences can be traversed in mentoring relationships if both parties are unafraid of facing up to their differences, are able to understand and acknowledge what matters to each other, and are mutually respectful and supportive. Indeed, difference can be a tremendous source for enrichment and learning, when mentors and protégés regard it as contributing to the lifeblood of the relationship rather than as an impediment to be dismissed, glossed over, or ignored.

During the many hours I spent interviewing my participants, listening, re-listening, and analyzing what they had to say, I repeatedly felt humbled and privileged to be given the opportunity to be a guest witness to their mentoring relationships. I was touched by the levels of warmth, caring, and concern that I experienced secondhand from these relationships. Living in a world where violence, unkindness, and self-interest seem to dominate the media and our collective consciousness, it was at times a refuge and comfort for me to reflect on these pairs who genuinely and actively cared about each other. These relationships give me hope and confidence that individuals can transform each other, and that the process of transformation can ripple out to communities, institutions, and society at large.

I wrote this book to distill and pass on the magic of my mentor's mentoring. I also hope that this book, in its own humble way, will encourage people to mentor, support the formation of positive relationships between diverse people, and contribute to greater understanding, appreciation, and respect for cultural differences.

Few of us can leave huge bequests when we hit the end of the road. However, we can *all* leave a legacy of kindness, generosity, and compassion when we become mentors. Those we mentor will likely continue the cycle of giving, thus perpetuating the good we initiated, perhaps indefinitely. In my view, this would be a pretty cool legacy in and of itself.

So . . . in the words of Joe, my mentor, I invite you to *pass it on.*

References

Angelou, M. (1998). Retrieved June 4, 2009, from http://thinkexist.com/quotes/maya_ angelou/

Angelou, M. (2008). *Who mentored Maya Angelou?* Retrieved March 1, 2009, from http://www.hsph.harvard.edu/chc/wmy2008/Celebrities/maya_angelou.html.

Auden, W. H. (n.d.). Retrieved June 1, 2009, from http://quotationsbook. com/quote/19816/

Boyle, P., and Boice, B. (1998). Best practices for enculturation: Collegiality, mentoring, and structure. In M. S. Anderson (ed.), *The experience of being in graduate school: An exploration* (pp. 87–94). San Francisco: Jossey-Bass.

Carruth, G., and Ehrlich, E. (1988). *The giant book of American quotations.* New York: Gramercy Books.

Chambers dictionary of quotations. (1997). New York: Chambers.

Chan, A. (2008). Best practices of outstanding mentors in psychology : an ecological, relational, and multicultural model. *Dissertation Abstracts International.* (UMI No. AAT 3313810)

Cook, J. (1993). *The book of positive quotations* (2nd ed.). Minneapolis: Rubicon Press.

de Bruyn, E. H. (2004). Development of the mentor behavior rating scale. *School Psychology International, 25*(2), 185–192.

Hardy, K. V. (2009). When "them" becomes "us." *Psychotherapy Networker* 33.

Henderson, J. (2007). *Cooked.* New York: William Morrow.

Johnson-Bailey, J., and Cervero, R. M. (2002). Cross-cultural mentoring as a context for learning. *New Directions for Adult and Continuing Educatio, 96,* 15–26.

Liu, E. (2004). *Guiding lights: The people who lead us toward our purpose in life.* New York: Random House.

The Merriam-Webster dictionary of quotations. (1992). Springfield, MA: Merriam-Webster.

Mortenson, G., and Relin, D. O. (2006). *Three cups of tea.* New York: Penguin.

143

Obama, B. (2008). *A more perfect union.* Retrieved June 1, 2009, from http://www
.msnbc.msn.com/id/23690567/.

Perez, J. (1993). The proactive mentor: Suggested strategies. *ADFL Bulletin* 24(2),
39–44.

"Quotable" quotes: Wit and wisdom for every occasion. (1997). Pleasantville, NY:
Reader's Digest.

Rogers, M. R., & Molina, L. E. (2006). Exemplary efforts in psychology to recruit and
retain graduate students of color. *American Psychologist, 61*(2), 143-156.

Tallchief, M. (1999). *National medal of arts.* Retrieved May 29, 2009, from http://
clinton4.nara.gov/textonly/Initiatives/Millennium/capsule/tallchief.html.

Thomas, D. A. (2001). The truth about mentoring minorities: Race matters. *Harvard
Business Review* 79, 99–107.

Thomas, D. A., and Gabarro, J. J. (1999). *Breaking through: The making of minority
executives in corporate America.* Boston: Harvard Business School Press.

Washington, D., and Paisner, D. (2006). *A hand to guide me.* Des Moines, IA:
Meredith Books.

Winter, S. (1977). Rooting out racism. *Issues in Radical Therapy* 17, 24–30.

Index

About the Author

Anne Chan, PhD, is a mentoring and diversity consultant. Her passion for mentoring was ignited when she found a caring mentor who guided her through her entire PhD program at Stanford University. Although she and her mentor came from entirely different worlds, they got along so well that she decided to focus her dissertation research on outstanding mentors who reach across cultural differences. Dr. Chan's mission is to teach and inspire people to be excellent mentors. When she is not busy consulting, researching, and writing about mentoring and diversity, she enjoys homeschooling her active son. Her website is www.mentoring4diversity.com